Praise for *The Secret of Literacy*

This book needed writing. Literacy, the quoin of education, has frequently been assumed, glossed over or ignored. Threaded through our personal and professional lives, it takes a brave soul to unpick it, unpack it and sort it. And that's what David Didau has done.

I was talking to my daughter about why I was so impressed with this book. I was telling her about how, when he has asked his students to write, Didau writes too. 'Wow, that's amazing. Really powerful!' was her reply. And indeed it is. And that's what characterises this book. Beyond the sensible critiques of theory, the detailed examples for making literacy work at every level, is a man walking the talk.

One example: he makes the case that finished work often doesn't show the blood, sweat and tears that have gone into it. And he describes some of the blood, sweat and tears that have made him the master practitioner he is. Less than helpful feedback from an observation, his response to it and his nuanced practice in relation to, for example, teacher talk. Another example in this vein: a group of NQTs observing one of his lessons where students are responding and challenging one another. And he is on the sidelines, with just the odd bat thrown in. Otherwise, they are just getting on with it. High quality conversations about their learning. But, as he says, this was not particularly helpful for the NQTs because they had not seen the struggles and the practice to get the students to this place. The point about this is that there are no easy, off-the-shelf answers. What there is, is practice, on the right things, continually refined.

Another example: modelling. Students critique his work alongside theirs. And in a mixed ability group how does he make sure that lower attaining students are getting the most out of it? Beautifully. He has them working alongside him as teacher's assistant. He also manages to get the reluctant to get involved too. Not by forcing them. But cracking on with it anyway.

There is so much here. He makes the case for difficult, compelling texts, brimming with knowledge. And these are opened up through scaffolding and skilful questioning. There's an incisive critique of low level scaffolding tasks. And this sets the scene for learning, which is characterised by high impact and low threat, and gets to grips with stuff that really makes a difference to the acquisition and love of language. It is sophisticated stuff, but it is also elegantly simple. Anyone reading this book and using any one of the things Didau discusses, would become a better practitioner.

One of the most powerful things for me was the realisation that some of our students who have pupil premium funding actually need some of the additional intervention and rich support which is now provided to EAL students on the best programmes.

And all of this is referenced against some serious thinkers and bloggers: Vygotstky, Dweck, Berger, Willingham, Hirsch, Robinson, Curtis, Kirby.

And he makes the case for the lower profile aspects of literacy – there's a very good summary of Robin Alexander's distinction between social and cognitive talk. And that means high quality talk from the teacher. There is a beautiful example of the pose, pause, pounce and bounce. If every teacher, in every school, across the country read page 77 and did this once a week, then progress, achievement, motivation, love of learning, all the cliches would increase. Guaranteed. How could they not? Really important that he paused on the pause and reminded us of the importance of thinking first before getting those ideas out.

And he holds us to account, too, in terms of the contribution our own language has on expectations. Shifting from clauses that include 'but' and replacing them with 'and'. I'm not going to say more, because it's important people read the book for the impact this shift has. At its heart, our role as professionals must be to open the door to academic games (in the Wittgensteinian sense), not dodging the difficult. And he shows how to embrace etymology. If this sounds daunting, in Didau's hands it isn't. There's the potential for masses of play here. In my experience all students of all abilities and backgrounds love this aspect of language development. Light years away from peeling posters of technical vocab on the wall.

It was good to see that he had also included the importance of high quality school libraries. There's only one aspect which I think could be developed further and that is the auracy dimension of literacy. The poorest of poor relations. He does explore it, but I think there is the potential for more. But given the man's genius at unpacking the rest of this essential entitlement for all students, it would have been a corker. In fact he's probably got another book in him about this.

The bottom line is that this book not only makes literacy explicit, it brings it to life in all its spirited messiness. My father, dour Scot, head of English in Peckham, word-monger of the first order, would have loved it. Can't think of higher praise.

Mary Myatt advises, writes and inspects, www.marymyatt.com

As an avid reader of David's brilliant blog I was really excited to read his new book. I wasn't disappointed! In his inimitable style, David manages to enliven and illuminate literacy, making what is a potentially tricky topic accessible and downright intriguing. He distils a shed-full of research and combines this with practical pedagogy.

David puts the compelling argument that literacy is not a bolt-on job for English teachers, but it is, rather, a fundamental aspect of great teaching in every lesson for all teachers. He dispels some enduring myths and establishes a clear, usable methodology that all teachers can instantly understand and apply in the classroom. There is a fantastic array of practical ideas and sharp insights which will mean this book is a great addition to the library of all teachers.

Every teacher should pick up this book – just watch out if you are a PE teacher!

Alex Quigley, subject leader of English and
assistant head teacher, Huntington School, York

The Secret of Literacy is an essential book for all teachers and school leaders. It is not just another literacy book. David Didau provides a crystal clear rationale for all teachers taking responsibility for developing literacy in their specialist areas, with lots of very practical ideas, drawing on a range of sources from blogs and the latest literature on the issue. Anyone familiar with David's own superb

Learning Spy blog will immediately recognise some of his most powerful ideas and his inimitable style: it is witty and accessible, grounded in the reality of everyday classrooms, but also conveys a sense of urgency. This is a serious business and, as David highlights, too much of what we do in the name of literacy isn't literacy at all. The book is challenging us to do better and shows us how. 'Making the implicit explicit' captures the key message, but *The Secret of Literacy* is more than a set of tools; it is a call to arms!

Tom Sherrington, head teacher, King Edward VI Grammar School, Chelmsford

David Didau's book is everything a book about the work of teaching should be: clear-eyed, lively, wise and funny. Written by a front-line practitioner of the craft. And best of all, reading it will make you better.

Doug Lemov, managing director, Teach Like a Champion Team

The Secret of Literacy

Making the implicit explicit

David Didau
@LearningSpy

 Independent Thinking Press

First published by

Independent Thinking Press
Crown Buildings, Bancyfelin, Carmarthen, Wales, SA33 5ND, UK
www.independentthinkingpress.com

Independent Thinking Press is an imprint of Crown House Publishing Ltd.

Quotes from Ofsted documents used in this publication have been approved under an Open Government Licence. Please visit www.nationalarchives.gov.uk/open-goverent-licence.htm

Page 79, figure adapted from John Sayer's deeper questions grid: Questioning, John Sayers Geography Blog http://sayersjohn.blogspot.co.uk. Pages 113-116, extract adapted from Chris Curtis's blog post: Deep Reading: Literacy Across the Curriculum, Learning from My Mistakes http://learningfrommymistakesenglish.blogspot.co.uk. Pages 128-132, extract adapted from Alex Quigley's blog post: Reading Fast and Slow, Hunting English http://www.huntingenglish.com. Pages 175-177, extract adapted from How to Start on Teach First: English © Joe Kirby, 2013

Megaphone image © aeroking - Fotolia.com

Images page 81 © Margarita Borodina - Fotolia.com, © gdvcom - Fotolia.com, © Robert Kneschke - Fotolia.com. Image page 82 © nyiragongo - Fotolia.com. Images page 101 © misu - Fotolia.com, © keller - Fotolia.com. Image page 108 © nuwatphoto - Fotolia.com. Image page 143 © pinselfee - Fotolia.com. Image page 194 © adore - Fotolia.com

British Library Cataloguing-in-Publication Data

A catalogue entry for this book is available from the British Library.

Print ISBN 978-178135127-7
Mobi ISBN 978-178135181-9
ePub ISBN 978-178-135182-6
ePDF ISBN 978-178135183-3

Printed and bound in the UK by
Gomer Press, Llandysul, Ceredigion

For Rosie – the star to my wand'ring bark.

Acknowledgements

I'm painfully aware of teacher and basketball coach, John Wooden's observation that 'The worst thing about new books is that they keep us from reading the old ones.' There are an awful lot of great books on literacy already out there and, if you want to find out more, most of them are well worth your time.

For those of you determined to read it, this book is the culmination of all the research and planning I have put into thinking about and designing the kind of literacy policy I've always wanted to have in place: one that was simple, supportive and useful.

When I started my role as director of literacy and English at Clevedon School I had, shall we say, an incomplete understanding of what a decent policy might look like. If the ideas in this book are any cop, then it's mainly down to such talented, thoughtful and generous practitioners as Geoff Barton, Chris Curtis, Joe Kirby, Kerry Pulleyn, Alex Quigley and particularly Lee Donaghy, who explained the ins and outs of genre pedagogy to me. I'm also indebted to Dee Murphy at Priory Community School for modelling how a decent literacy coordinator approaches the role. And while we're at it, special thanks must go to John Wells and Jim Smith at Clevedon School for all their encouragement and for basically letting me get on with it.

I'm also extremely grateful to Caroline Lenton at Crown House for giving me the green light, Phil Beadle for being polite about it, Bev Randell for making sure everything ran smoothly and Emma Tuck for her considerable forbearance, and for making me look better than I am.

Acknowledgements

Special thanks must also go to Tom Fitton and Pete Jones for thrashing out the design of a cover that I actually liked. This was no mean feat.

Finally, I need to thank Chris McPhee at Teachology for allowing me to develop the ideas contained herein into something approaching coherence during a series of day courses, which some people kindly said they quite liked.

Contents

Contents

Contents

Introduction

For there is nothing either good or bad, but thinking makes it so.

Shakespeare, *Hamlet*

This is not a book (just) for literacy coordinators or school leaders; it is a book written with every teacher in mind. In many ways, this is much more a book about teaching than it is a book about literacy and I very much hope that whatever and whoever you teach, you will find something useful within. But that said, I make no claims that it contains 'the answer' to teaching, or teaching literacy or anything else, merely that it contains some possible answers. It's important to keep in mind there's nothing that's always going to work for every teacher in every context. Having said that, everything that I've included has been road-tested either in my own teaching or that of my colleagues and, to that extent, can be said to 'work'. But don't take my word for it: find out for yourself. Teachers are inundated with 'how to' manuals and this leads us to forget the importance of *why*. Whatever you decide to use, I'd urge you to think carefully about the why. What do you hope to achieve? Because there are no magic bullets. As long as you have approached what you plan to do with sufficient thought, it will probably work. If you haven't, it probably won't.

And therein lies a problem: a lot of literacy teaching is done unthinkingly. Perhaps the biggest barrier to teaching literacy well is the word itself. 'Literacy' is a bit off-putting, isn't it? Yes, of course we all know what it means, it just sounds a bit too solemn and scientific. Primary schools were forced to get cosy with it after the introduction of the Literacy Hour back in the 1990s. Kids suddenly started having literacy lessons and you might think that this would have solved the problem of what exactly the word means, but as far as I can tell it's only muddied the already murky waters. My own daughters are currently in Years 4 and 5 and appear to be taught a confusing combination of literacy, phonics and grammar. Quite how literacy has become distinct from phonics and grammar I have no idea, but it's certainly the case that the very mention of the word stirs up anxiety about our lack of grammatical knowledge, and sounds unutterably and appallingly tedious. Few words demand demystification as much as this one. The problem, in a nutshell, is that 'literacy' sounds like it's someone else's problem.

One way to deal with the problem of the word is not to use it. Maybe we could stop thinking about embedding the teaching of *literacy* in our lessons. We could try calling it language, or maybe just plain old teaching and learning instead. Because it isn't an optional extra. Developing reading, writing and oracy are (or should be) absolutely fundamental to every teacher's approach to pedagogy; teaching pupils to read, write and communicate is not something special that you need to do on top of your job. It *is* your job! But more than that, the subject you teach, whether it's science, geography, maths or, dare I say it, PE, has its own language. Your pupils will primarily understand your subject through reading or listening and primarily demonstrate their understanding through writing or speaking.

But that's not really the secret I want to share with you. The *real* Secret of Literacy was unearthed by head teacher and literacy guru, Geoff Barton, after long years of tireless study and patient experimentation.[1] He's been generous enough to share it with me and, in turn, I want to entrust it to you because this secret is something rare and precious; once you know it, it will change everything. Your teaching will, quite simply, never be the same again.

The Secret of Literacy is … making the implicit explicit.

I can almost hear the groans of disappointment. It's what?

Having waded through our degrees, we teachers are a fairly literate lot. Even you PE teachers have to write a dissertation, don't you? (It's not all running and

---

1   Geoff Barton, *Don't Call It Literacy! What Every Teacher Needs to Know about Speaking, Listening, Reading and Writing* (London: Routledge/David Fulton, 2013).

catching, you know!) This means that, whether we know it or not, we have an implicit understanding of how to communicate successfully. We know how to speak in a variety of different social situations and we don't ever have to think too much about how we actually do it, we just do it. But because we've never really had to think about *how* we communicate, this means that we're often not very good at explaining to the uninitiated how to go about doing what we find (relatively) easy to do. Our problem is that we don't always know how to make our knowledge explicit, so that others can do what we can do.

That, my friends, is where I come in. The greater part of this book is about providing you with simple, straightforward strategies which will enable you to make the implicit explicit, so that your pupils will have a greater chance of succeeding in a world where the ability to communicate in a variety of media is becoming more important.

The good news is that, as far as schools and teachers are concerned, there's no such thing as literacy. Yes, you heard me. In a book on the subject, I'm contending that literacy is a meaningless chimera and should be consigned to the hell occupied by such evils as SEAL (Social and Emotional Aspects of Learning) and PLTS (Personal Learning and Thinking Skills). Just saying this is a wonderful catharsis. There is no such thing as literacy. There is just good teaching and learning.

This does, however, make the job of the literacy coordinator somewhat problematic because most teachers are crying out to know what it is they're supposed to be doing, and just telling them it doesn't exist is unlikely to go down well. This book is an attempt to show that 'literacy as a thing' is a bankrupt concept and ought to be avoided at all costs. The pernicious but worryingly prevalent idea of the bolt-on literacy objective and the content-free literacy activity needs to be taken out and shot at dawn. Instead, the secret I want to share with you is that teaching literacy cannot be usefully separated from teaching subjects. What that means is the knowledge of a subject is the language of the subject.

It's useful to remind ourselves that beating our heads against a desk to produce resources which, if anyone ever bothers to use them, will make very little impact on pupils' ability to communicate better, is an exercise in pointlessness. Instead, my approach to literacy is that it should have high impact on pupils but require low effort in terms of planning and implementation. Or, to put it another way, we should do the bare minimum required for all teachers to understand and be able to discharge their responsibilities as teachers of English.

What's that you say? All teachers? Teachers of English? Nah, mate, you've got the wrong bloke. I teach [*insert subject here*], I do. You won't catch me mucking around with no literacy in me lessons. That's what the English department's for, innit?

Well, I'm here to tell you that, contrary to some of the opinion bubbling in shadowy staffroom corners, improving pupils' literacy is part of the professional responsibility of every teacher: 'If you're a teacher *in* English, you're a teacher *of* English. We cannot give a lesson in any subject without helping or neglecting the English of our pupils.'[2]

The bad news for dissenters is that this simple piece of homespun wisdom is now enshrined in the Teachers' Standards which clearly state that all teachers must, and I quote, 'demonstrate an understanding of and take responsibility for promoting high standards of literacy, articulacy and the correct use of standard English, whatever the teacher's specialist subject.'[3]

So that's that. You've gotta do it. The Department for Education has fashioned a huge stick to beat teachers about the head and neck with. You *will* teach literacy, or else!

Despite the rumours, I'm not all about wanton bullying and striking fear into the hearts of PE teachers. (Before we proceed any further, I feel it's important to make clear that PE teachers tend to take literacy teaching very seriously and are amongst the most enthusiastic, if not downright competitive, of all teachers in their desire to raise literacy standards. That said, they're an easy target and I will continue to make cheap jokes at their expense.)

No, I see my mission as inspiring folk to understand why they should want to embrace the challenges of improving the life chances of the little blighters in our

---

2 George Sampson, *English for the English: A Chapter on National Education* (Cambridge: Cambridge University Press, 1921), p. 25.

3 Department for Education, *Teachers' Standards* (May 2012). Ref: DFE-00066-2011. Available at: <https://www.education.gov.uk/publications/eOrderingDownload/teachers%20standards.pdf>, p. 7.

care. Because, let's face it, whether you believe it's all about exams or not, children's life chances are only going to be improved by being literate.

But it's not just that you *should* teach literacy; the bigger issue is that you *are* teaching literacy, whether you like it or not. The only question is: are you doing it badly or well? This means that at some point, in every lesson, you will be modelling how to read, write, speak or listen. And you'll either be providing an admirable model, or you won't. This being the case, surely it's well past time to ensure that we're doing our jobs to the best of our ability.

Ever since Ofsted upped the ante on reading and literacy, schools have been scrabbling around producing policies so as to be seen to be doing something. Anything. But, if what you do doesn't show impact in the classroom then it's a complete and utter waste of everyone's time and effort. My advice, therefore, is to concentrate on those high impact, low effort strategies which will give every teacher the opportunity to show that they are teachers of the literacy that drives the content they are teaching. It almost goes without saying that the more you do for someone the less they value it and, conversely, the more someone does for themselves the more valuable it becomes. I've seen scores of literacy coordinators in schools all over the country who work their socks off producing reams of spelling starters, punctuation posters and grammar guides which no bugger ever uses. This simply cannot be a good use of anyone's time. Much better to shift the emphasis onto equipping teachers (and therefore pupils) to do it for themselves.

Now, despite this harangue, you might be feeling that literacy really isn't that important in your subject area and that, willing as you are, there really isn't much scope to promote the correct use of Standard English in your average maths lesson. Well, you'd be wrong. In the vast majority of lessons, pupils are asked to read stuff and then write it down. And even in those where printed materials and pens are seldom seen (PE, again), there is almost always a requirement that pupils listen, if not speak. I defy you to conceive of a lesson that, deliberately, involves none of the above. You can't, can you?

This means that every single lesson is a golden and unmissable opportunity to take responsibility for doing all that the Department for Education says you should be doing. And if you're not *actively* teaching pupils how to better use the academic language they need to access your subject, then you're ensuring that the gap between the haves and have-nots will only get wider.

Chastening, isn't it?

Chapter 1
Why is literacy important?

It's not (just) because Ofsted say so!

In the world of the current Ofsted inspection, few schools will quibble with the prominence being given to the teaching of literacy. But I'm far from convinced that we're clear on precisely *why* teaching literacy is so important, beyond the fact that Big Brother is watching.

The effect of 'affect'

For those of us fortunate enough to be literate, the whole idea of literacy in schools can seem bewilderingly overcomplicated. Something that comes to us as naturally as breathing can hardly require all the fuss and bother devoted to it, surely? Reading and writing can appear so straightforward that there *must* be something wrong with those who struggle.

But, if we're able to resist the temptation to label those with poor literacy as somehow deficient and thus attribute biological or social causes for their shortcomings, we might have more of a chance of addressing some of the real issues. One of the most fascinating of these is the effect of *affect*. How we feel about a thing determines, in large part, how good we will be at that thing. The feeling of struggling with reading and writing can create a sense of searing anxiety. For the most part this tends to be portrayed as the result of failure: 'We always describe anxiety as the cart, but it could just as easily be the horse. Anxiety could just as easily be a primary cause of failure rather than its result. It could, at least beyond the very initial stages of literacy failure, be prior to, rather than consequent upon, this failure.'[1]

When I was at school, I decided early on that I was bad at maths. I found manipulating numbers tricky and this made me feel stupid. When given a maths problem to solve I would become anxious, and the more anxious I became, the harder it was to concentrate on the numbers. It got to the point where I would feel that I was having a panic attack.

Unsurprisingly, I decided that it would feel far more comfortable not to try. And so I gave up. I spent the remaining years of maths lessons doodling, staring out of the window and generally avoiding doing any work. It was easier to give up and resign myself to being rubbish at maths than it was to deal with the crippling anxiety of making an effort and failing. Teachers shrugged and shunted me down the sets until I found myself largely untroubled and left to my own devices in the bottom set. My teachers' expectations of me were as low as those I had for myself. Equally unsurprisingly, I got a D grade in my GCSE maths exam.

I didn't care. I left school blithely convinced that I was bad at maths, and who needs to know any of that stuff anyway?

Some years later I decided I wanted to be an English teacher. No problem. I had a decent English degree and a variety of universities were happy to take me. Except that I needed a C grade in maths. I railed against the injustice of this and howled 'why?' at the moon before buckling down and enrolling in an evening class.

This was probably the single most difficult and painful episode I have ever endured. I wept bitter tears of frustration at the improbabilities of probability and almost tore out my hair at grid references. I just didn't get it. Who was I kidding? There was no way I could ever pass the damn thing; I might as well give up. In my desperation, I even considered paying someone to sit the exam for me.

But something in me persevered. I got hold of some past papers and, with the help of a friend, did one of them every day for the month before the exam. If I started to bug out, I would just skip the question and focus on the ones I could do. And,

---

1   Hugo Kerr, *The Cognitive Psychology of Literacy Teaching: Reading, Writing, Spelling, Dyslexia (and a Bit Besides)* [ebook]. Available at: <http://www.hugokerr.info/book.pdf>, p. 77.

as I got used to the processes of solving equations and translating shapes, my anxiety began to fade and I started to recognise that I could do it. On the day of the first exam I experienced a moment of pure joy as I realised that I knew the answer to *every single question on the paper!* I didn't have to miss out any of them. The second paper didn't go quite as perfectly but I was still pretty sure I'd done well.

When, a few months later, I went to collect my results I actually managed to feel disappointed that I had *only* got a B! This was back in the days when there was an intermediate tier for maths GCSE and a B was the highest grade it was possible to get. I can't tell you how proud I felt. This was the first time in my life that I had accomplished something that I hadn't found easy. It was, I realised after beginning my PGCE course, great preparation for the rigours of teaching.

Anyway, that lengthy and self-indulgent anecdote does have a point. There's lots to infer about the importance of mindset, and it certainly taught me that I could achieve anything, if I was prepared to put in effort despite the discomfort of failing. But, more than that, it has allowed me to empathise with those pupils who 'can't do' English. Although reading and writing have always come so easily to me, I know what it's like to feel stupid and to believe that I can never get better.

Those who struggle with their literacy feel the same anxiety about their deficiencies as I did about mine. And my story is both a cautionary tale and a cause for hope. The debilitating anxiety felt by so many pupils when asked to read or write chimes so absolutely with my own experience: emotions affect performance. They affect the enjoyment of learning and they also affect the work we are able to produce. Obviously, this can also be a huge benefit: I have always got a huge kick out of studying language. Because I so actively enjoy reading and writing, my performance of these skills is also joyful.

The Matthew Effect

For whosoever hath, to him shall be given, and he shall have more abundance: but whosoever hath not, from him shall be taken away even that he hath.

Matthew 13:12

In his excellent book, *The Matthew Effect*, Daniel Rigney sets out a stark message. He points out that, 'the word rich will get richer while the word poor will get poorer'.[2] There are two main reasons for this. Firstly, 'while good readers gain new skills very rapidly, and quickly move from learning to read to reading to learn, poor readers become increasingly frustrated with the act of reading, and try to avoid reading where possible'.[3] Who can argue with that? Few people persevere with something they find difficult and uncomfortable. No one wants to feel stupid, and struggling to read is guaranteed to make you look thick. If you're literate you will gravitate towards literate friends. It comes as no surprise that 'good readers may choose friends who also read avidly while poor readers seek friends with whom they share other enjoyments'.[4] And these friendships make a difference. The more we interact with the word-rich, the deeper our own pool of words will be. Because, as Myhill and Fisher point out, 'spoken language forms a constraint, a ceiling not only on the ability to comprehend but also on the ability to write, beyond which literacy cannot progress'.[5] So, if our spoken language isn't up to snuff nothing else will be either. This advantage means that those 'who possess intellectual capital when they first arrive at school have the mental scaffolding and Velcro to catch hold of what is going on, and they can turn the new knowledge into still more Velcro to gain still more knowledge'.[6]

---

2   Daniel Rigney, *The Matthew Effect: How Advantage Begets Further Advantage* (New York: Columbia University Press, 2010), p. 76.

3   Daniel Rigney, *The Matthew Effect*, p. 76.

4   Daniel Rigney, *The Matthew Effect*, p. 76.

5   Debra Myhill and Ros Fisher, *Informing Practice in English: A Review of Recent Research in Literacy and the Teaching of English* (London: Ofsted, 2005), p. 4.

6   E. D. Hirsch, Jr, *The Schools We Need: And Why We Don't Have Them* (New York: Anchor Books, 1999), p. 20.

Success breeds success, and our confidence and enthusiasm will be bolstered, further stoking our expectation that we can succeed again in the future. When we struggle, we don't consider ourselves to be failures. Instead, we'll put this down to the complexity of a text. The more difficult a task, the keener we'll be to attempt it, and our motivation becomes intrinsic.

But this is not the case for many. It's all too easy to write off 'kids like these' as thick and having no hope of achieving anything. The pressure on pupils to be literate is enormous and failure is usually attributed to something inherent in a child. This kind of labelling and negative language is toxic.

This leads inexorably to the same learned helplessness I used to feel when encountering numbers. Interestingly, this 'mathematics anxiety' is well known and has been knocking about in academic literature since the 1970s. But 'literacy anxiety' hasn't had the same kind of coverage.

And, as you're no doubt aware, poor literacy results in some shocking statistics:

- One in six people in the UK struggle with literacy. This means their literacy is below the level expected of an 11-year-old.

- Seven million adults in England cannot locate the page reference for plumbers in a telephone directory.

- One in sixteen adults cannot identify a concert venue on a poster that contains the name of the band, price, date, time and venue.

- More than half of British motorists cannot interpret road signs properly.[7]

So there it is. We practise what we're good at and we're good at what we practise. If the problem starts with poor reading skills then so must the solution. As Robert Macfarlane says, 'Every hour spent reading is an hour spent learning to write.'[8] This is only becoming more pressing as increasingly 'the digital world is centred

---

7   Statistics are taken from Deeqa Jama and George Dugdale, *Literacy: State of the Nation: A Picture of Literacy in the UK Today* (London: National Literacy Trust, 2010).

8   Quoted in Literary Non-Fiction: The Facts, *The Guardian* (21 September 2012). Available at: <http://www.theguardian.com/books/2012/sep/21/literary-nonfiction-the-facts>.

around the written word'.[9] As teachers we need to know that if we're not explicitly addressing the needs of the have-nots, then the gap between the word-rich and word-poor will grow ever wider.

So whose fault is it?

Well, apportioning blame never really helps, but it's interesting to note that at age 7, children in the top quartile have 7,100 words whilst children in the lowest quartile have less than 3,000.[10] At this age we could argue that the main influence is parents. But one study shows that at age 16, one in twelve children have a 'working vocabulary' of around 800 words.[11] Whose fault is that?

Could *we* be responsible? Even if we're not, there's no one else who can, or who will, help the word-poor. It's up to us. But are we up to the task?

Anecdotally, I hear that many teachers struggle with their own literacy and, obviously, this will be a barrier in their roles as teachers of English. So, what to do? As professionals we have a duty to do something about our own standards of literacy. And clearly schools have a duty to provide training that helps address this problem. Ofsted say in *Removing Barriers to Literacy* that, 'in the secondary schools where teachers in all subject departments had received training in teaching literacy … senior managers noted an improvement in outcomes across all subjects, as well as in English'.[12] So this is about enlightened self-interest as much as anything else.

---

9   European Commission, *EU High Level Group of Experts on Literacy: Final Report* (September 2012). Available at <http://ec.europa.eu/education/literacy/resources/final-report/index_en.htm>, p. 26.

10 Andrew Biemiller, Vocabulary: Needed If More Children Are To Read Well, *Reading Psychology* 24(3–4) (2003): 323–335, at p. 327.

11 Aislinn Laing, Teenagers 'Only Use 800 Different Words A Day', *The Telegraph* (11 January 2010). Available at: <http://www.telegraph.co.uk/education/educationnews/6960745/Teenagers-only-use-800-different-words-a-day.html>.

12 Ofsted, *Removing Barriers to Literacy*. Ref: 090237. Available at: <http://www.ofsted.gov.uk/resources/removing-barriers-literacy>, p. 7.

Ofsted also say:

> [S]chools need a coherent policy on developing literacy in all subjects if standards of reading and writing are to be improved. Even with effective teaching in English lessons, progress will be limited if this good practice is not consolidated in the 26 out of 30 lessons each week in a secondary school that are typically lessons other than English or the 70% or so of lessons in primary schools that do not focus on English.[13]

This would seem entirely reasonable. If you're going to have a policy of developing literacy, why not make it a coherent one? And if pupils' reading, writing and oral communication is only valued in 30% or less of their lessons then it's little surprise if they've got the message that these things are not that important. It's become clear to me that what we practise we get good at. It would never occur to me not to use capital letters when writing even the scrappiest of notes. I just do it. Likewise, when many of our pupils write formal essays, it doesn't occur to them to use capital letters. Not because they don't know how to, and not because they're lazy. It's because they've practised not using them and have become really good at it.

The O Factor

Depressing as it is to reduce such things to a checklist, I'm sure it will be of more than passing interest to most teachers to know what it is that inspectors will be looking to see in their lessons. Helpfully, Ofsted have published a list of what they're looking for:

- Are key terms and vocabulary clear and explored with pupils to ensure that they recognise and understand them? Are they related to similar words or the root from which they are derived?

- Do teachers identify any particular features of key terms and help pupils with strategies for remembering how to spell them or why they might be capitalised (e.g. 'Parliament' in history or citizenship)?

....

13 Ofsted, *Moving English Forward*. Ref: 110118. Available at: <http://www.ofsted.gov.uk/resources/moving-english-forward>, p. 31.

- Do teachers remind pupils of important core skills – for example, how to skim a text to extract the main elements of its content quickly or to scan a text for information about a key word or topic?

- Do teachers make expectations clear before pupils begin a task – for example, on the conventions of layout in a formal letter or on the main features of writing persuasively?

- Do teachers reinforce the importance of accuracy in spoken or written language – for example, emphasising the need for correct sentence punctuation in one-sentence answers or correcting 'we was … ' in pupils' speech?

- Do teachers identify when it is important to use standard English and when other registers or dialects may be used – for example, in a formal examination answer and when recreating dialogue as part of narrative writing?

- Do teachers help pupils with key elements of literacy as they support them in lessons? Do they point out spelling, grammar or punctuation issues as they look at work around the class?

- Does teachers' marking support key literacy points? For example, are key subject terms always checked for correct spelling? Is sentence punctuation always corrected?[14]

I have to say that this is setting the bar rather low. We can and should all be doing these things routinely. It helps to remember that if we're not teaching literacy well, we're teaching it badly.

Real solutions are as simple to identify as they are difficult to implement:

- If a pupil is struggling with literacy, assume that this is a combination of anxiety and learned helplessness rather than a deficiency.

- Have high expectations of all pupils – even *those* kids.

---

14 Ofsted, *Reading, Writing and Communication (Literacy): Distance Learning Materials for Inspection within the New Framework*. Ref: 110125. Available at: <http://www.ofsted.gov.uk/resources/reading-writing-and-communication-literacy>, pp. 43–44.

- Give pupils a taste of success at reading and writing. This involves making tasks hard enough not to be easy, but not too hard that they won't be able to manage to complete them without minimal support.

- Make the implicit explicit: teach pupils the reading and writing strategies others take for granted.

This is all a lot easier said than done, but with an unswerving belief that intelligence is not fixed, and with deliberate practice and the power of positive language, it might be possible to alter the crippling anxiety many of our pupils experience on a daily basis.

Academic register: the language of power

Literacy is a bridge from misery to hope.

Kofi Annan

Hopefully it's not going to come as any great surprise that academic register has nothing whatsoever to do with attendance. One of the most intractable barriers to many pupils' chances of success is the vast gulf between the language they speak at home and the language of school or, as it's more usefully labelled, academic register. This mismatch lies at the core of the underachievement of many word-poor pupils. These pupils are only able to use their 'everyday' language to navigate the school curriculum but, as we all know, academic subjects draw on different kinds of language to make their meanings. Sadly, unless we want to dumb down the curriculum to a point where it's completely valueless, it's impossible to penetrate the meanings of academic subjects using everyday language. Predictably, these pupils don't tend to do well at school.

EAL (English as an Additional Language) pupils have it especially tough; no matter how much support they get in their native tongue at home, they won't get much mileage out of using it to make meanings in school. Less obvious, but equally problematic, is the variation in language used between word-poor pupils and the academic language of school subjects. Often we fail to recognise the difficulties encountered by some word-poor pupils as being related to language; their difficulties are more likely to be blamed on motivation, behaviour or attitude. If we recognise that the issues faced by EAL and underachieving, disadvantaged pupils are often language related, we might be able to do something about it by explicitly teaching them the academic language they need to succeed at school.

One of the fundamental premises of this book is that explicitly teaching academic literacies is an essential task for schools and teachers. Those of us who grew up speaking and writing it at home are at a huge advantage. Teaching Standard English as a foreign language to speakers of other dialects is vital if they are to have a fair chance in life. Whether we think this is fair hardly matters; the harsh reality is that if children don't know how to write correctly and speak Standard English, society will judge them as 'thick'.

The first step is to get teachers to know and understand the importance of academic literacies. When teachers know about the language of their subject they are in a position to teach their pupils how to learn within these subjects, principally through reading, and also to demonstrate their learning within these subjects, principally through writing.

If we're serious about addressing the problems caused by the Matthew Effect, we need to develop pupils' language skills so they are able to read and write academic language across all subjects. To do this we need to understand the academic language of our subjects and the role language plays in effective learning. We also need to teach the academic literacy of our subject explicitly.

Objections

OK, we're convinced: literacy is vital to pupils' life chances. The next hurdle to vault is that of anxiety. The overwhelming majority of teachers are just crying out to do something positive to improve pupils' literacy but have a few very real concerns which must be addressed.

● **I'm not an English specialist – what the hell should I do and what if I get it wrong?**

This is very common and brought about because many teachers are uncomfortable with their own lack of grammatical knowledge. They worry that teaching literacy will be all about subordinate clauses, past participles and the Oxford comma, whatever that might be. But whilst it may well be worth expending some energy on improving teachers' literacy, it's important to acknowledge that all teachers are (or should be) highly literate. They managed to get degrees and, as such, they will have a decent implicit ability to read, write and speak. This must be harnessed.

● **This literacy stuff is all very well but I've got a subject to teach**

Again, true. Teachers must not be made to feel that they ought to cobble together ludicrous bolt-on literacy objectives which remove the focus of the content they're struggling to cover. You really can't 'do' the science and then 'do' the literacy; they're inseparable. Our job is to find the literacy within our subjects and make explicit our expectations of how pupils will read, write and speak in a way that they will better understand the lessons we're teaching.

● **You've already made me rewrite my schemes of work to include PLTS, SEAL and every other numpty initiative to trundle along in the past few years – I'm just too knackered to start writing them yet again**

Quite. '[I]f you want a sure way to provoke a collective groan in your staff-room, announce that you are intending to hold a training day devoted to whole-school literacy. "We did that five years ago," someone will shout.'[15] Literacy cannot be 'done'. But, generally speaking, teachers work quite hard enough. Our approach to literacy needs to demand low effort on the part of the teacher, but have an immediate and clear impact on pupils. It's no good messing about creating loads of well-meaning worksheets and PowerPoints that no one's ever going to use.

With this in mind, what follows are practical suggestions that have been thoroughly road-tested, and that every teacher can, quickly and easily, add to their teaching repertoire and use in every lesson where pupils are expected to use language. So, that said, I'm going to suggest some steps for developing a culture of literacy in your lessons that are high impact and, wherever possible, low effort.

----

15 Geoff Barton, Whatever Your Subject, You Are a Teacher of English, *Times Educational Supplement* (5 March 2010). Available at: <http://www.tes.co.uk/article.aspx?storycode=6038152>.

Chapter 2

The teaching sequence for developing independence

Independence is happiness.

Susan B. Anthony

The teaching sequence

If we want our pupils to use academic language confidently and independently, then we need to think carefully about what sequences of lessons should look like. I've always believed that great teaching and learning happens in cycles or loops, and I've been furiously honing my ideas on what I think might be the ideal teaching cycle. After much research, thought and experimentation, I've decided it looks something like this:

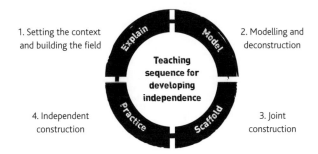

Source: Adapted from Susan Feez, *Text-Based Syllabus Design* (Sydney: McQuarie University/AMES, 1998).

We start by explaining a new concept, its subject-specific vocabulary and how it connects to those things pupils have already learned. When this exposition is complete and pupils' basic understanding is secure, we then move on to demonstrating, Blue Peter style, a model of how this concept might be applied and deconstructing the ways in which it was put together. Once these processes are clear, we can then move on to providing a scaffold to enable pupils to apply the knowledge they have learned. Then, when pupils have achieved a minimum standard of control over these processes, we can allow them, with clear guidance and feedback, to practise independently. And finally, when they have mastered the skill they have practised, it is time to connect new concepts and increased complexity; the cycle begins again.

It should be clear that no part of this sequence is really possible without any other part. If you've failed to explain the concept you wish pupils to learn, then they will be confused and quickly become lost. If you don't explicitly model how to apply this new knowledge, then the process will remain mysterious; some will pick it up but many won't. Neglecting to scaffold throws pupils in at the deep end before they're ready to swim. The arm bands offered by a competent teacher provide a much-needed feeling of safety and equip pupils with the ability to take risks within a safe environment. Not allowing pupils to practise prevents them from encoding the knowledge they've learned, and the opportunity to transfer concepts from working to long-term memory is missed.

This may seem obvious, but it doesn't reflect the way many teachers feel they are expected to teach. Or perhaps it does; increasingly, it has become an expectation that each part of this cycle should be (briefly) included in one 50–60 minute lesson. The madness inherent in believing that learning takes place in neat, lesson-shaped chunks has resulted in the four-part lesson, the Ofsted lesson and the reluctant acceptance that if we want to please observers we must perform the Monkey Dance™ and conceal the (essential) parts of our teaching that certain people seem not to approve of. Skipping over the fundamental need to explain, model and scaffold in order to demonstrate the 'preferred' Ofsted method of minimal teacher talk and independent learning for its own sake may have done more to damage children's education than any other single diktat.

It is my contention that whilst you may not always want or need to cover just one of these four elements over the course of a single lesson, there may equally be times when it is necessary. As Graham Nuthall tells us, 'learning takes time and is not encapsulated in the visible here-and-now of classroom activities.'[1] That being the case, we need to allow pupils the time they need by providing them with the rich, fertile soil of excellently crafted lessons devoted to each part of the cycle. There must be an acceptance that any and all of these four types of teaching can be considered outstanding when done well. Currently, teachers fear teaching lessons described variously as didactic, teacher-led or 'from the front'. This must change. We need to allow teachers to teach and, by extension, children to learn.

Part of the solution is designing lessons, and sequences of lessons, around a teaching and learning cycle which promotes the development of pupils' control over language and which will result in true independence. At certain points in this cycle it's important for teachers to shut up and let pupils practise applying the skills and knowledge they've learned, but at other times it's essential that we instruct our classes effectively.

This cycle provides a model for ensuring that our talk makes the strongest possible impact on pupils' ability to write, speak and think in academic register.

Stage 1: Explain[2]

Explaining a joke is like dissecting a frog. You understand it better but the frog dies in the process.

E. B. White

The first stage of the sequence is dependent on you (the teacher) being able to explain clearly and coherently whatever it is you want your pupils to know. I say

1 Graham Nuthall, The Cultural Myths and Realities of Classroom Teaching and Learning: A Personal Journey, *Teachers College Record* 107 (2005): 895–934, at p. 922.

2 Some of the ideas in this section have been adapted from Alex Quigley's blog post: Explanations: Top Ten Teaching Tips, *Hunting English* (11 May 2013). Available at: <http://www.huntingenglish. com/2013/05/11/explanations-top-ten-teaching-tips/>.

'know' here quite deliberately. I realise that knowing things is a bit fuddy-duddy and most writers of education books would probably prefer you to concentrate on getting pupils to *understand* instead. And of course I'm all for that. The problem is that understanding is ephemeral. I've lost count of the number of occasions when, after an inspired lesson, a class has understood the concept I've wanted them to learn clearly and completely, only to have forgotten it by the time I see them next. What then is the point of understanding something you can't remember? Much better to concentrate on making sure pupils can remember first and understand second. You haven't taught until they've learned.

There are some definite pitfalls to avoid in explaining things to kids. The biggest criticism of teachers talking is that it's boring. And, generally speaking, boring pupils is not a good way to get them to learn stuff. But to suggest that teachers should therefore avoid explaining their subjects to pupils is a bizarre leap. Surely it would be vastly more sensible to expend our efforts in improving teachers' ability to explain?

This then is our aim: how can we make our explanations better?

The starting point in teaching any new concept or idea is to lay the groundwork of the propositional knowledge required. This type of transmission lesson is deeply unfashionable and is something that many teachers are at pains to conceal. We all know that sometimes the most effective way to teach children is to talk to them, although we must always be wary that if they're not learning, we are just talking.

So then, what makes a great explanation? I'm going to argue that for an explanation to work it has to be clear, memorable and relevant. And, ideally, it should also try to avoid killing the frog.

Building the field involves the introduction of new language and concepts, whereas setting the context is about placing this new topic within the framework of what your pupils already know. This is the 'why' of the area of study and it needs to come first if pupils are going to be able to make relationships between new information and existing information. Hence, the first chapter of this book explains why I think literacy matters before going on to model and scaffold some practical advice on how to go about teaching pupils to use academic language.

So, if I wanted to teach you about beds, I would start by giving you the names for the component parts (mattress, headboard, base, etc.) before explaining a little bit about their history, different varieties of bed (futons, hammocks, bunk beds, etc.) and a brief summary of their cultural importance.

Thankfully, I'm not going to bore you further about beds. Instead, here are three principles which should fit all great explanations: they should be clear, memorable and relevant.

Clear

If an explanation is precise enough, it is a lever capable of moving the world. But to be able to clearly explain a complex concept takes thought and planning. Explanations should be pitched so as to be not too complex as to be unintelligible, but not too simple or unchallenging that pupils don't really learn anything. Ideally, your language will be adapted to activate links between what they already know and what you're trying to teach.

It's useful to remember that what's clear to us may not be so obvious to our pupils. Wittgenstein's duck/rabbit puzzle is a useful way to visualise this.

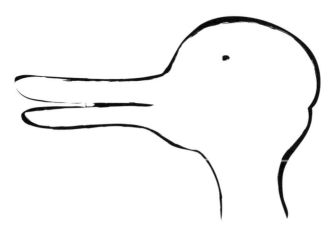

Ludwig Wittgenstein's duck/rabbit puzzle

There have been plenty of occasions when I've tried to show my pupils a duck, for them only to be able to see a rabbit. Often the cause is that my own understanding is a little shaky. If I, as the teacher, am unclear, it's unlikely my pupils will follow my explanation. This is a clear illustration of the need for excellent subject knowledge. As Einstein may or may not have said, 'If you can't explain it simply, you don't understand it well enough.'

One way I rely on to ensure my explanations are clearer is to break down the components of what I want to teach and to give pupils the language they need to explain it. It might seem easier to describe the circulatory system as 'very fine tubes' but it's far more useful to call them capillaries. My best advice here is to make sure you use the specialist academic language used by experts as often and as clearly as you can. And insist that pupils use it too. What we practise we get good at, so if we allow them to practise using sloppy, imprecise language, that's what they'll get good at.

Of course, there's a fine line between talking over pupils' heads and baffling them with irrelevant jargon and talking down to them. Of the two, I'd rather err on the side of complexity. I'd rather they were forced to change their thinking by incorporating new terms into the schema they are developing than leave them with something so slimmed down it's almost stripped of meaning.

Questioning

So, you've tried to be as clear as possible, but has it been clear enough? An essential component of being clear is checking that pupils have followed your explanation. There is no better way to ensure that your explanation sticks then by questioning. The simplest way to do this is by asking questions that clarify, probe and recommend (see pages 70–71).

But be mindful, though, about why you're asking questions. If they don't make your explanation clearer, maybe this is not the right time. Obviously, if I'm asking questions to clarify then it ought to follow that this should result in pupils being able to articulate their understanding.

Subject-specific language

In most explanations there are one or two important key words that we want to stick in pupils' minds. Just teaching inert vocabulary isn't enough; we also need to show how these terms form the academic language of our disciplines so that pupils can discuss new concepts with confidence and authority.

In a maths lesson we might want pupils to learn such language as quadratics, numerators, coefficients and polynomials. In English they might be expected to learn alliteration, pathetic fallacy, motif and characterisation. In science there's conservation, photosynthesis, nucleotides and refraction. These are just the tip of a very large iceberg. If these terms (and the host of others pupils are expected to know) are to have any chance of being retained, they need to be used and embedded in our explanations.

If pupils are going to be able to produce high quality academic writing, then they need to practise speaking like this. And the best way to begin this practice is to see and hear you as a subject specialist using it in your explanations.

Concrete examples

Most of what we want pupils to learn is pretty abstract and the more abstract a concept, the harder it is to grasp. Pity the poor child who has up to 12 different subjects to hold in their mind, and also consider that at times these different subjects provide different explanations of the same concept. For instance, 'structure' means something very different in science, history and English.

Happily, an abstract concept becomes much easier to understand when we're able to provide concrete examples to illustrate our meaning. We need enough examples to be able to share a concept so that pupils are gonna remember it and, hopefully at some point, understand it. So if you want to explain a concept like onomatopoeia (I didn't have to look it up!), fractions or the respiratory system, you need to prepare a whole host of concrete examples to illustrate these concepts in advance. Then ask pupils to compare the differences and similarities. Once they've had a chance to do this, give a clear definition and then give them yet more examples to apply to this definition.

Ideally, explanations should include non-examples as well as examples. Sometimes we can understand a concept best by seeing what it *isn't*. So, if we provide 'crackle', 'drip', 'splatter' and 'whoosh' as examples of onomatopoeia, and 'explosion' as a non-example, pupils should start to have a pretty good idea of what the concept might mean.

Another potential pitfall is that if the examples we provide are ambiguously similar, then pupils might misunderstand the concept we're trying so desperately to explain. For instance, if I wanted to explain the concept of 'green' and showed you pictures of four different green apples, you might very well fail to understand what I meant. I'd do much better to show you pictures of an apple, a green car, some grass and a green traffic light; the chances that my explanation has been misunderstood are now minimised.

Or, if we were only to provide example of fractions with 1 as the numerator ($\frac{1}{4}$, $\frac{1}{2}$, $\frac{1}{3}$), pupils may get the idea that fractions are always less than one. If we want to avoid this misapprehension, providing some examples where the value of the fraction is greater than 1 could be useful ($\frac{9}{8}$, $\frac{12}{3}$, $\frac{7}{2}$).

We are more likely to remember concrete knowledge than abstractions. We are hardwired to do this. When we learn a language, we begin with concrete nouns and then move on to verbs to articulate our most basic needs.

Memorable

If pupils don't remember what we teach, then they haven't learned. We've all experienced corking lessons where everything seems to go right and pupils *really* understand the tricky concepts we need them to learn, only for them to have forgotten it all next lesson. This being the case, we will benefit from working on ways to make our explanations more memorable.

Here are some suggestions that might help.

Appeal to feelings

Although an emotional response will make what you say more memorable, we should be wary of a 'style over substance' performance. Getting the balance right between engagement and learning is a delicate process; just because pupils enjoy your lessons doesn't mean they're learning. Relate your explanations to what they already know (your concept maps are invaluable here) and, for goodness' sake, make it personal – tell stories about your own experiences and those of others; a well-chosen anecdote can often open up an otherwise abstract concept.

Analogies and metaphors are crucial to language, thinking and memorising. Our minds naturally draw upon schemas (the existing patterns of knowledge we have to help us learn new knowledge). To make new knowledge memorable, we need to find a way to attach it to existing schemas. We draw on our prior knowledge to make sense of new information. These comparisons give pupils helpful templates to build on their prior knowledge and allow them to make educated guesses.

This might be as simple as relating the rules of lacrosse to the rules of hockey, or it might be as elaborate as using the Salem witchcraft trials of the 18th century to illuminate Senator McCarthy's hounding of communists in the 1950s.[3]

Memorable anecdotes bring facts alive; dry statistics are enlivened when turned into a story. If 63% of pupils achieving A grades in an exam is pretty interesting, it isn't nearly as memorable as the story of an individual toiling to overcome tough circumstances in order to gain that grade. Our minds make meaning by creating stories. In history we imagine and empathise with particular 'characters'. Our explanations therefore need to be constructed as narratives – with characters, conflicts and resolutions.

Cognitive scientist, Daniel Willingham, contends that lesson content is full of potential conflicts or 'big questions'. This is basically the same as working out the structure of your lesson and turning it into a narrative with rising action, a climax and falling action. He suggests reverse engineering the material we want pupils to learn and considering what questions it might prompt. He gives us this example of teaching about the different models of the atom that were proposed during the

....

3   Oops! I think Arthur Miller may already have this one covered.

20th century. The obstacle to students understanding is that the results of different experiments appear to contradict each other. The conflict seems to be resolved with each new model that's proposed but then new complications are generated. Instead of focusing on the facts, there's a ready-made narrative to explore here. A teacher mindful of the need to make explanations memorable would do well to unearth the points of conflict in the 'story' of the atom.[4]

Structuring lessons in this way is interesting (and therefore motivational) but also makes the content more memorable. In this way, pupils will be hooked by the actual substance of the discipline. As Dylan Wiliam points out, 'Getting students engaged so that they can be taught something seems much less effective than getting them engaged by teaching them something that engages them.'[5] The idea that the content of our lessons needs to be made relevant to pupils is hugely problematic. A Shakespeare sonnet, quadratic equations and Hinduism are not necessarily going to seem relevant to many pupils – does that mean we should avoid teaching this stuff? Of course not. Instead, it means working out the narrative or point of conflict within these topics so that we can get pupils to think about big, important questions.

Compare and connect

Whether you want to explain the effects of varied paragraphing, Pythagoras' theorem, osmosis or the Treaty of Versailles, it's vital to compare the new concept you're teaching to ones that pupils will already be familiar with. But this doesn't mean we should use *The Simpsons* to teach *Macbeth*, or the Mr Men to teach the rise of the Nazi Party. This isn't just about dumbing down (although you may have a view on that); it's more that if Daniel Willingham is right that 'memory is the residue of thought',[6] then we must ensure our comparisons make pupils

---

4   Daniel Willingham, *Why Don't Students Like School? A Cognitive Scientist Answers Questions About How the Mind Works and What It Means for the Classroom* (San Francisco, CA: Wiley, 2009), p. 85.

5   Dylan Wiliam, *Embedded Formative Assessment* (Bloomington, IN: Solution Tree Press, 2011), p. 10.

6   Willingham, *Why Don't Students Like School?*, p. 54.

think about the ideas we're trying to teach. If they don't think about it, they won't remember it.

So, if I want pupils to understand the plot of *Macbeth*, it won't help them to be thinking about Marge and Homer instead. If I want pupils to understand how the leaders of the Nazi Party came to power, making them think about Mr Silly and Mr Grumpy will only be a distraction. These activities may (or may not) be 'fun' or 'active', but they're not a useful way to explain what you actually want pupils to know because they won't remember what you want them to remember. In one of my most memorable biology lessons at school, my teacher knocked over the model skeleton (it's the law that at least one lab per school must contain a full-size model skeleton) and told us that we'd remember the lesson for the rest of our lives. I have. But I cannot for the life of me recall what the lesson was about.

Our analogies should help pupils construct a schema into which they can fit new ideas. So, if I was an IT teacher trying to explain the concept of a firewall I might use the analogy of a bank clerk. In this analogy, a website is a bank; if I want to get my money out of the bank they're not usually keen on me rummaging around in the vaults and helping myself. Instead I have to ask the clerk. The firewall does a similar job; if I want to access a secure site on the Internet, I have to be allowed through the firewall first. This analogy is helpful because it relates a new concept to an existing one without me wasting a lot of time thinking about banks and money; it helps me think about websites and firewalls better.

There's nothing worse than banging on for too long, except perhaps not saying enough. A great explanation should be structured in such a way that the likelihood that pupils remember what you want them to remember is increased. If your core message is featured in the language of the lesson outcome, it will have maximum exposure: you'll tell them what they're going to learn, they'll learn it and then you'll tell them what they've learned. Hey presto! A three-part lesson in its purest form.

And repeat ...

It's also worth knowing that if information is to be retained in long-term memory we need to revisit it. That being the case, a great explanation needs to be followed up if we want it to stick. Ebbinghaus's forgetting curve is a handy reminder that our core message should be subject to spaced repetitions, or else it will be forgotten.

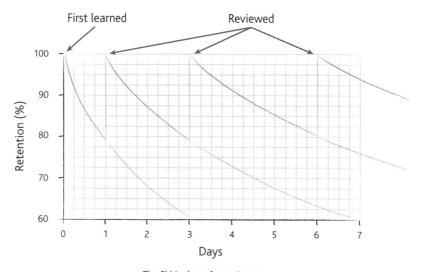

The Ebbinghaus forgetting curve

Relevant

This isn't an argument for being 'down with the kids'. What I mean by relevance is that what we explain to pupils should be necessary for them to know; it should lead logically from what they have already understood.

Even if an explanation is clear and memorable, sometimes it won't take root simply because it's not relevant. This is all about sequencing ideas and building up a knowledge base (or schema) one step at a time. There's little chance that even the best explanation of sentence structure is going to make sense if pupils aren't clear on what a verb is, and it's unlikely that they'll understand why Brutus decided to kill Caesar if they have no idea about the formation of the Roman Republic.

So our explanations need to be carefully sequenced. Generally, spending time on explaining the context of an idea is time well spent. I guess it's possible to fall down a rabbit hole here and go too far back, and possibly it might seem depressingly utilitarian to limit our explanation to what we think pupils 'need to know'. But at some point this is precisely what we must do. It seems self-evident to suggest that explanations should 'start at the beginning', but often this isn't possible. As experts, we are required to determine where our explanation should begin and the vital steps from there on.

The Kevin Bacon Game, or Six Degrees of Separation (see pages 157–158), is a useful way to get pupils to reflect on the explanations we've offered. The idea is that they need to logically sequence their understanding from one concept to another. So we might ask them to suggest the six degrees of separation between the assassination of Archduke Ferdinand and the outbreak of the Great War, or between Pip's first meeting with Magwitch and his discovery that he has 'great expectations'. To keep them on track, we might specify that step 4 must be the introduction of Mr Jaggers, or the Ottoman-German Alliance or whatever. And if six degrees is too few or too many then feel free to extend the chain as far as you think it should stretch.

Know what your pupils know

Explanations will be much more relevant if we know what our pupils already know. Assessing prior knowledge is one of the master teaching skills. How on earth can we ever hope to have a sense of what has been learned if we're ignorant of what was already known? Graham Nuthall worked out that 40–50% of what we teach is already known by our pupils. And to make matters worse, this knowledge is likely to be unique to individuals, with everyone in the class possessing a largely exclusive fund of prior knowledge. What in the name of all that's holy do we do with *that*?

What pupils already know about the subject their teacher is teaching

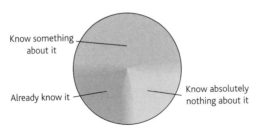

Source: Adapted from Graham Nuthall, *The Hidden Lives of Learners*
(Wellington: New Zealand Council of Educational Research, 2007), p. 35.

Well, you give them a test to see what they already know or you could have them draw out a concept map of their knowledge and understanding that they'll add to throughout the scheme of learning. If pupils are made to map out what they know on a subject in a clear and ordered manner, you can clearly see what they know from the outset. If you compare these initial maps, pupils can be grouped to capitalise on what they already know; misconceptions can be shared and no one feels like what they already know is being ignored. New learning is added to the map and related to existing knowledge logically, so that at the end of a unit of work it should be clear that everyone has arrived at the intended outcome. Without this kind of assessment, your wonderfully crafted explanations will often fall on stony, infertile ground. But if you begin by knowing what your pupils know, all will be well.

Additionally, you need to know when pupils have misunderstood the explanation you've been giving. In a perfect world, our explanations will be so clear and well-designed that everyone will understand them 100% of the time. Back in the real world, we're only human and sometimes our fumbling best isn't good enough. Concept maps (or any other type of testing) will allow us to identify misunderstandings and provide timely, corrective feedback before those misunderstandings become too deeply encoded.

Solid explanations are essential if we want pupils to be able to express abstract and unfamiliar concepts in anything other than broken, inarticulate approximations. Understanding requires us to know the words. If you don't have the language to describe a thing, then what really can you know about it?

So, once we've built the field and set the context for the wondrous learning we want to pass on, pupils are ready to deconstruct models that will set them on their way to arriving at their own independent meanings.

Stage 2: Model

Part of teaching explicitly is taking on the role of coach and using the principles of observational learning in demonstrations. Teachers do this all the time, but do we do it well? If it was possible to simply watch an expert demonstrate a process, we could all become excellent teachers just by watching videos of each other. Just watching a demonstration is, of course, not enough. Good modelling includes a commentary where we break down complex processes into simple steps, provide time to check understanding and make sure pupils have opportunities to ask questions.

Deconstruction

Deconstruction, or 'having a bloody good look', as it's more affectionately known, involves seeing how things work. Everyone remembers the science lesson in which they dissected a frog, or a bull's eye or whatever it was; the purpose was to see how the ultimate 'expert' had put living organisms together. Sadly, most of the lesson I remember was spent fainting or giggling maniacally whilst waving mangled corpses in the faces of anyone who hadn't fainted yet.

But, if better managed, this process of induction will help pupils understand the principles of a device, object or system through an analysis of its structure, function and operation. Sounds frighteningly technical? Fortunately, it's actually very simple. Learning a new concept by observing exemplars happens constantly, whether it's a baby learning a new word or an electrician categorising an electrical fault.

In English, an essential part of the teaching sequence for writing has always been to deconstruct texts to work out how they were constructed. It ought to go without saying that pupils will be better writers if they've had the opportunity of seeing what good writing looks like.

Here is an example I've used in the past to demonstrate the techniques a writer might use to build a sense of menace or tension:

> An awful self-destructive curiosity pulled Peter closer. Unable to stop himself, he got down on his hands and knees and crawled the final few inches towards the grave. As he approached, something else caught his attention. There was a hole in the soil, at the head of the grave, near the cross. The hole was about the size of a small fist, and perfectly circular, like a rat hole in a river bank.
>
> Peter leant over it.
>
> He looked in.
>
> There was just enough light to see inside the hole.
>
> At the bottom he saw an eye.
>
> It was open, seemingly lifeless, though looking straight at him.
>
> Then it blinked.
>
> Peter screamed and ran as if the devil himself were chasing him.[7]

By deconstructing this passage, pupils were able to work out that by using very short sentences and paragraphs, the writer was able to drag out the moment of climax. This led to the realisation that full stops create pauses and that pauses slow the reader down. They were also able to see that the adjectives used in the first paragraph worked to increase tension by extending the moment of discovery. In other words, slowing down your reader is likely to make the writing more tense.

---

7   Marcus Sedgwick, *My Swordhand is Singing* (London: Orion Children's Books, 2007), p. 103.

And here's another extract we could deconstruct to examine the techniques used to convey action in a piece of writing:

> The mercenaries began to back away from the rebels, stabbing their spears fran-tically to try to create a gap between them and their enemies. As soon as some were clear they turned and ran towards Cato's men, immediately endangering their slower comrades as the rebels swarmed into the gaps in the rapidly fragmenting line. A handful were cut off and overwhelmed, attacked from all sides as they des-perately swirled around, trying to block the rebels' blows. Inevitably, a blade darted in, and as a man staggered back from the wound he was hacked to the ground in a flurry of sword blows and spear thrusts.[8]

From this, pupils were able to work out (with help) the following success criteria for writing effective action sequences:

● Use longer and varied complex sentences to help speed the reader up.

● Use powerful, exciting verbs.

● Use adverbs to describe action.

● Avoid using adjectives – they slow the reader down.

When teaching pupils how persuasive articles work, I've often resorted to some of the bad-tempered polemic easily available in online versions of daily newspa-pers.[9] These kinds of articles are great for exploring the techniques a writer might use to get attention and create humour. But whilst they may be perfect for see-ing how a writer uses language to argue, persuade and take the mick, it doesn't demand much in the way of content knowledge. I was, I now see, so concerned with teaching procedural knowledge (skills) that I 'forgot' to teach new proposi-tional knowledge (facts), relying instead on what pupils already knew about the world. Well, maybe I'm exaggerating slightly here, but it's all too easy to do this when insufficient time has been spent laying the groundwork and building the field that the pupils will need to study.

---

8 Simon Scarrow, *Centurion* (London: Headline, 2008), p. 78.

9 See here for an example: <http://www.mirror.co.uk/news/uk-news/mistargeted-dog-insurance-law-is-another-206967>.

How much more effort would it have taken to provide examples from Dickens or Hardy? How much more benefit might have been accrued if I'd used an article from *The Times* or *The Guardian* instead of the *Daily Mail?* The reason for not doing this, in the past, was that I believed it was sufficient to focus on the skill of writing and neglected many opportunities for enriching my pupils with some of the more challenging texts out there. As Matthew Arnold said, teaching should be about sharing 'the best of what has been thought and said' over our rich history. Not just what an entertaining tabloid journalist came up with last night.

But we don't want to just deconstruct written texts. In other subjects there will be other products you will want to deconstruct and whilst many of them will be written, many won't. The trick is to be clear about what it is you want your pupils to produce, find good quality real-world examples and reverse engineer them.

Modelling

It has been a great sadness to me that despite spending many hours watch Wimbledon over the years, my ability to play tennis hasn't improved. You would think that watching the world's best players would have made me a better player but regrettably, it turns out, we don't learn well from watching experts perform. If novices are to have a hope of learning to perform like an expert they need to have performance broken down into processes that can be considered and copied.

Science and mathematics have long traditions of model-making. Such modelling involves abstraction and simplification in order to better understand a particular feature of the world. In practical subjects, the model, be it a pencil case, drawing, cupcake or dance, will be created, Blue Peter style, by the teacher as an example of what success looks like. This is, of course, very useful. But of much more use is allowing pupils to observe the process of creation.

For years now I've made it a maxim that whenever I set pupils a task, I complete it too. Of the many benefits this has, one of the best is that I've built up a huge store of exemplar writing. Sadly, much of it was scribbled on paper and has been consigned to the great recycling centre in the sky, but much of it lives on in digital form. Not only is this useful to deconstruct, it has also provided lots of options for discussing my choices and reasoning. Sometimes it's enough just to see a model, but an essential part of the teaching sequence for writing is the process of modelling – talking through the decisions a writer makes at the point of writing. And the only way I know to do this effectively is to talk. I've written before about thinking like a writer, and the techniques of Slow Writing (see pages 161–165) lend themselves very well to effective modelling.

One of the most insurmountable barriers to independence is that many pupils tend to default to writing in everyday language. So, a powerful use of the modelling process is to show them how to make changes so that their writing is less like spoken language and more like academic language.

Take a look at this introductory paragraph to a history essay on the causes of the First World War:

> The causes of the First World War are more complicated than they look at first. Although the war started when Archduke Ferdinand was assassinated on 28 June 1914, the causes go back further than that. One thing that caused the war was that nations believed they were better than each other and so they behaved aggressively. Another cause was that countries like Germany, Britain and France all wanted to conquer parts of Africa. As a result, these countries all built up strong armies and navies. The final cause was the alliances that had been formed. Europe was divided between the Triple Alliance between Germany, Austria–Hungary and Italy and the Triple Entente between Britain, France and Russia.

As you can see, it's been written in 'everyday language' and as such is a bit clumsy; if it is to be a successful piece of academic writing we need to model how a historian might go about writing it.

Consider this improved paragraph:

> Although the Great War appeared to start with the assassination of Archduke Ferdinand, the causes are more complex. An increased sense of nationalism had led to aggressive posturing between nation states, which was worsened by the imperialistic desire of Germany to compete with the empires of Britain and France. This led to a militaristic arms race and culminated in the alliances formed between Germany, Austria–Hungary and Italy, and Britain, France and Russia, which left Europe poised on the brink of war.

The use of the discourse marker 'although' indicates that a qualifying point is to follow (see page 141) but the main difference is the introduction of nominalised factors. Nominalisation (the process of turning active verbs into passive concepts and ideas – see pages 87–88) makes writing more concise because so much meaning can be packed into these abstract concepts.

The deconstruction of high quality exemplars allows us to glimpse successful writing, but modelling allows the novice to access the thought processes of an expert. These processes are absolutely vital if we want pupils to become independent. Without expert, explicit modelling we have to rely on our implicit understanding. The word-rich will pick it up without ever being properly able to articulate how or why, and the word-poor will be buggered. And, in order for this to work, I'm afraid everyone just has to shut up and listen to sir.

In our rush to stop teachers talking we have prevented pupils from having a clear idea of what 'good' looks like. Instead we have relied on vague, bullet-pointed success criteria. Any teacher who uses success criteria that are unaccompanied by deconstructed exemplars and then explicitly modelled, is damning their word-poor pupils to never really knowing what it is they need to do to perform like an expert.

Stage 3: Scaffold

This is the stage of the teaching sequence that maybe most closely resembles the type of lesson that many people have understood as being preferred by Ofsted. It will probably include pupils working collaboratively and independently of their teacher. As such, this is perhaps familiar territory and possibly unnecessary to revisit. That said, I reckon that many joint construction lessons go wrong because of misunderstandings about why and how to scaffold tasks appropriately. Everyone benefits from scaffolding to help move from kind of knowing vaguely what to do, to being confident. Confidence is key; if we lack it then we're going to struggle to be independent.

Before examining some practical examples of how to do this, it's worth having a bit of a look at the underlying theory. And for that we need a nodding acquaintance with Lev Vygotsky's ideas about cognitive development. Amongst other things, Vygotsky argued that learning is social and happens by interacting with our environment.[10] He also thought that we need a 'more knowledgeable other' to help guide us through the complexities of this learning. This seems to suggest that we need both peer interaction and direct instruction if pupils are to make real progress.

The concept of the more knowledgeable other is closely related to the most well-known principle of Vygotsky's work, the zone of proximal development, or 'the distance between the actual developmental level as determined by independent problem solving and the level of potential development as determined through problem solving under adult guidance'.[11] Obviously, a pupil will achieve much more with guidance and encouragement than they might independently. Vygotsky saw the zone of proximal development as the area where the most sensitive instruction or guidance should be given to allow pupils to develop skills they can then use on their own. This has become synonymous with the concept of scaffolding, although apparently Vygotsky never used the term himself.

Unfortunately, scaffolding has become conflated with writing frames (and other harbingers of low expectation) and is consequently tarred with the same brush. It may be useful to use PEE (Point, Evidence, Explain), or one of its many variants, to get pupils to structure their writing, but these often result in formulaic writing which slavishly follows a structure with little understanding of the processes and thinking involved. The best scaffolding will support pupils' thinking and their ability to integrate new concepts, as well as providing a structure. But all too often scaffolding is used to make work easier. This is a mistake. Scaffolds should only be used to make it possible for pupils to do something they would find too difficult without support. If we pitch our expectations at the very top, and then scaffold upwards, we will not go too far wrong. We must have the same high expectations for all pupils, but understand that everyone will need a different level of support to achieve these expectations: same bar, different ladders.

....

10   Lev Vygotsky, *Thought and Language* (Cambridge, MA: MIT Press (2012 [1962]).

11   Lev Vygotsky, *Mind in Society: The Development of Higher Psychological Processes*, new edn (Cambridge, MA: Harvard University Press, 1978), p. 86.

Scaffolding can be defined as, 'Those elements of the task that are initially beyond the learner's capacity, thus permitting him to concentrate upon and complete only those elements that are within his range of competence'.[12] Or, to put it another way, if we do the bits that pupils can't, they will be able to tackle the bits they're ready to attempt successfully without getting distracted and frustrated. Ideally, scaffolding should include a mix of techniques:

- Offer general encouragement, e.g. 'Now you have a go.'

- Give specific instructions, e.g. 'Do this first, then try … '

- Directly demonstrate, e.g. showing pupils what to do.

Our job in the process of joint construction is to select which approach is best suited to particular pupils at any given time. This is a delicate balancing act made more complicated as whole-class instruction is almost impossible in those lessons where pupils are 'having a go.'

The process of scaffolding needs to:

- Get pupils interested in the task.

- Simplify the task sufficiently to allow pupils to attempt it.

- Give specific suggestions on how to approach the task.

- Deal with pupils' frustration at 'not getting it.'

- And, most importantly, challenge pupils to attempt a task that is just beyond their current level of competency.

Sounds exhausting, doesn't it?

Clearly, there's a lot more at work here than just plodding on with PEE. For scaffolding to be successful, teachers need to know their pupils really well. There is no substitute for having a clear picture of their prior attainment. This knowledge enables us to differentiate effectively and to ensure that scaffolding is successfully

....

12 David Wood, Jerome Bruner and Gail Ross, *The Role of Tutoring in Problem Solving* (Oxford: Pergamon Press, 1970), p. 90.

targeted at the area that will make the most impact on pupils' ability to be able to do something that is currently just out of their reach. The great thing about this is that it can look like marvellous progress is being made as rows of chipper children demonstrate an ability to do what previously they couldn't. If an observer comes in to see a successful lesson in the joint construction stage of the teaching sequence it can appear almost magical. The teacher doesn't appear to have to talk much and pupils seem to know enough to be able to get on with it. But this is a conjuring trick. As teachers we are often at pains to showcase this kind of lesson to impress observers, but pupils cannot learn by joint construction alone. It must be understood and accepted that this kind of lesson will only be successful once new concepts have been carefully explained and success has been expertly modelled.

Arguably, a contemporary application of Vygotsky's theories is reciprocal teaching. In this method, teacher and pupils collaborate in learning and practising four key skills: summarising, questioning, clarifying and predicting. The teacher's role in the process is reduced over time. Here's a handy bank of prompts you could use to help guide peer questioning:

- What is a new example of …?

- How would you use … to …?

- What would happen if …?

- What are the strengths and weaknesses of …?

- How does … tie in with what we learned before?

- Explain why …

- Explain how …

- How does …?

- What is the …?

- Why is …?

- How are … and … different?

- Compare … and … with regard to …

- What do you think causes …?

- What conclusions can you draw about …?

- Do you agree or disagree with this statement: …? Support your answer.

- How are … and … similar?

- How are … and … best … and why?

By scaffolding these questions, we can better structure the quality of group discussion whilst also honing pupils' meta-cognitive understanding and allowing them to actively make the next step in their learning. If pupils can be supported to ask better questions, we will make them better learners. And we all want that, right?

We can also see how Vygotsky's theories feed into models of collaborative learning, suggesting that group members should have different levels of ability, so more advanced peers can help less advanced members operate within their zone of proximal development. Some might call this effective differentiation. Others might call it a waste of 'more able' pupils' time. I couldn't possibly comment.

For me, one of the most effective ways of scaffolding pupils' ability to think is to prompt them to shift their speech from everyday language to academic register. As we've seen, pupils who seem incapable of putting anything down on paper are not necessarily being lazy; it may be that they just don't have the words. For experts, shifting from everyday to academic language is seamless. As soon as I think a thing, I am able to 'translate' it into the formal code required for academic writing. I don't even notice I'm doing it. For some word-poor pupils this transition is seemingly impossible. But prompting them to use Thought Stems (see page 83) to scaffold this transition from thought to speech to writing is almost magical. As soon as you've said it, you can write it. If we want pupils to be able to work independently, we can improve their ability to write by using scaffolding at the point of speech.

That said, there are still times when it is useful to use a writing frame to scaffold writing. There are many and various graphic organisers we can use to help pupils structure their writing (see pages 120–121) but one of the most overlooked issues with these tools is that the scaffolding is left visible. If we are going to put up a scaffold, we need to have a plan for taking it down again. If we were to build a house, as soon as building work is completed the scaffolding would be removed. But all too often pupils' writing resembles a rural Greek landscape, marred by ugly scaffolding left to rust visibly.

In the essential guide to great writing, *The Elements of Style*, master rhetorician William Strunk offers this advice:

> Vigorous writing is concise. A sentence should contain no unnecessary words, a paragraph no unnecessary sentences, for the same reason that a drawing should have no unnecessary lines and a machine no unnecessary parts. This requires not that the writer make all his sentences short, or that he should avoid all detail and treat his subjects only in outline, but that every word tell.[13]

There are a great many stock phrases in general use which make writing baggy and add extraneous grammatical garbage. Special ire is reserved for the stock phrase 'the fact that'. I'm ashamed to report that while proofreading this book I found about 20 instances of this phrase, which I promptly deleted.

When we teach pupils to write academic essays, we give them scaffolds that contain stock phrases. These phrases are the glue that hold their thoughts together and provide their work with structure. But often the phrases become redundant. Students continue to use them long after their usefulness has been exhausted. Consider such gems as 'The first point I am making is …' or 'The writer is using the phrase … because …' These can be essential as pupils first learn the basics of essay writing but quickly become clunky with overuse. However, it's very difficult to know when and how to remove this scaffolding.

---

13 William Strunk Jr, *The Elements of Style* [ebook] (n.p.: Tribeca Books, 2011 [1918]), loc. 31.

Black space

The idea of using 'black space' came after a conversation with English teacher, Kay Tinsley. Her approach to redrafting written work is to get students to use a marker to black out what she calls 'the redundant chunk'. This immediately struck me as good advice.

Consider this extract from a pupil's essay on *Julius Caesar*:

> Act 3 scene 2 is important because Brutus lets Antony speak to the people of Rome which is the turning point of the play. Antony makes what could be the best persuasive speech in English literature. It fits into the play because before Antony's speech Cassius persuades Brutus to join the conspiracy to kill Caesar. Brutus then lets Antony speak at Caesar's funeral because he trusts him: 'I know that we shall have him well to friend'. This shows that Brutus is wrong to trust Antony because he turns the people of Rome to his side and gets them to riot. Antony says, 'Cry havoc! And let slip the dogs of war'. This shows that he is deliberately making the people riot.

The scaffolding is jarringly visible: the writing and the pupil both appear less impressive than they might. To improve it we need to black out anything that isn't absolutely essential to the meaning of the paragraph:

> Act 3 scene 2 is important because Brutus lets Antony speak to the people of Rome which is the turning point of the play. Antony makes what could be the best persuasive speech in English literature. It fits into the play because before Antony's speech Cassius persuades Brutus to join the conspiracy to kill Caesar. Brutus then lets Antony speak at Caesar's funeral because he trusts him: 'I know that we shall have him well to friend'. This shows that Brutus is wrong to trust Antony because he turns the people of Rome to his side and gets them to riot. Antony says, 'Cry havoc! And let slip the dogs of war'. This shows that he is deliberately making the people riot.

Clearly, it no longer makes sense and requires redrafting.

> The turning point of the play comes when Brutus lets Antony speak to the people of Rome. Before Antony's speech, Cassius persuades Brutus to join the conspiracy to kill Caesar. Brutus allows Antony to speak because he trusts him: 'I know that we shall have him well to friend'. Brutus is wrong to trust Antony. The line 'Cry havoc! And let slip the dogs of war' shows that Antony wants revenge and intends to turn the people of Rome to his side and get them to riot.

This last example has greater lexical density, is more economical and expresses the writer's thoughts with more sophistication. Less is more. And that's it: lexical density in action. The power comes not only from pupils actively blacking out their own scaffolding. The acres of black space help them to see just how much of what they write is unnecessary. What's more, it's a very efficient way to give feedback. Embrace the power of black space.

Vocabulary continuums[14]

One way to make scaffolding minimally intrusive is to use vocabulary continuums. If we want to encourage pupils to express their thoughts with greater nuance we could ask them to come up with alternative words of descending or ascending intensity along a continuum like the one below:

So, if pupils found themselves writing something along the lines of, 'Romeo feels sad when he believes that Juliet has killed herself'. We might need to explore alternatives for 'upset':

By adding words, pupils can tweak the inference they are making to arrive at a more precise understanding of what a writer is trying to convey.

---

14 These ideas were suggested by Professor Mary Schleppegrell at a lecture on functional grammar I attended at Aston University. You can find out more about her fascinating work at the University of Michigan at: <http://www.soe.umich.edu/people/profile/mary_schleppegrell/>.

We could also use a 'probability continuum' to help pupils understand tentativeness when making a claim in an argument:

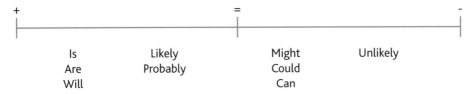

So, instead of simply making bald assertions, pupils can begin to explore modality with a scaffold that is easy to remove because it is straightforward to internalise.

The ever-present danger of scaffolding is that pupils may become over-reliant on our support, therefore, we must always keep in mind the consideration of when to withdraw support.

Here is a checklist of issues to consider when using scaffolding:

- Will the scaffold support pupils to begin to complete increasingly challenging tasks independently?

- Can you scaffold at the point of speech or does it need to be written?

- How will you make sure pupils do not become reliant on the scaffold?

- Does the scaffold encourage formulaic writing?

- What is your plan to get rid of the scaffold so that it's not visible in the final draft of work?

As soon as pupils have internalised the structures and knowledge needed to construct independently, we need to move on to Stage 4 of the teaching sequence.

Stage 4: Practice

Practice makes permanent; only perfect practice makes perfect.

At this point you should, if you've talked effectively, be able to finally zip it. We are finally ready for true independent work, where pupils are confidently able to transcribe their thoughts without having to speak because of all the high quality talk to which they've been exposed. This is in sharp contrast to what often gets passed off as 'independent learning' in the name of reducing teacher talk.

My mum spent a good deal of my childhood telling me that practice makes perfect and that if I was ever to amount to anything then I needed to crack on with whatever it was she wanted me to be good at. Well, it turns out that my mum was wrong: practice doesn't make perfect, practice makes permanent. What we practise we get good at. And sometimes we get very good at doing things badly.

Take writing for instance. When I scribble notes I always use capital letters correctly. This isn't a boast, I just do. It would never occur to me not to, I don't even think about it. When I read pupils' work they invariably omit capital letters for proper nouns. Now, I rarely meet a secondary pupil who is unaware of where capital letters should be used, and if you point out that they missed some, then they generally know exactly where to put them. I used to think this was laziness, but I realise now it's not. They're doing exactly what I do: unthinkingly repeating what they've practised. After years of practising, they have become superb at not using capital letters. And it takes a real effort of will to remember not to do something we do unthinkingly. This is what Doug Lemov calls 'encoding failure',[15] and it is best avoided if we're serious about pupils mastering the skills and knowledge we're teaching them.

The independent construction stage of the teaching sequence is one of those areas of teaching that has become hidden. I've often heard teachers say something along the lines of, 'Oh, don't come and watch that lesson – they'll just be getting on with it' or, 'They're just doing an assessment, there's no point you observing because I won't be doing any teaching.' I think this is a little odd. Surely, can there be a

---

15 Doug Lemov, Erica Woolway and Katie Yez, *Practice Perfect: 42 Rules for Getting Better at Getting Better* (San Francisco, CA: Jossey-Bass, 2012), pp. 26–27.

better way of demonstrating progress and independence than by seeing a class of kids working in silence? It certainly doesn't happen accidentally. If pupils are sufficiently confident to be able to work without the teacher's help, then they must have been really well taught.

Part of the reluctance behind wanting to be seen presiding over this kind of lesson is that some teachers aren't sure what to do with themselves. Obviously, drinking coffee and surfing the net are not going to appear particularly constructive. And I understand that. I'm pretty sure I'd baulk at taking this approach even though one could argue that it might be perfectly justifiable.

But often the demands of covering content and a lack of curriculum time mean we don't give pupils nearly enough opportunities to practise. We tell ourselves (and them) that it's all about 'skills' which they should be able to transfer from one subject to another. But if they don't get the chance to master these skills in one area before being asked to jump through new, slightly differently shaped hoops then they are never going to be able to transfer them. The point of practice is to achieve mastery.

For those who worry that 'mastery' might be an unattainably giddy height to which mere mortals cannot aspire, let's quantify and distil the term to something on which we can agree. Mastery is not perfection; it's just being really good at something. Gladwell's bastardisation of Ericsson's work into the neat figure of 10,000 hours may not be in any substantive way true,[16] but it is a useful way of looking at mastery. There isn't a short cut. Mastery, however we define it, takes time. But (and this is the good news) if we want it enough, if we're prepared to put in the effort, mastery is achievable.

....

16 See Malcolm Gladwell, *Outliers: The Story of Success* (London: Penguin, 2008) and K. Anders Ericsson, Michael J. Prietula and Edward T. Cokely, The Making of an Expert, *Harvard Business Review* (July–August 2007). Available at: <http://www.uvm.edu/~pdodds/files/papers/others/2007/ericsson2007a.pdf>.

Growth mindset and grit

We must begin with the determination to work towards mastery and the belief that, with hard work, amazing things are possible. The process of explaining, modelling and then scaffolding ought to have prepared pupils for this. If it hasn't, you may need to revisit some of the steps. Part of our job is to convince any particularly truculent or apathetic pupils that (a) they can, and (b) they should work towards a goal. 'Mastery' may seem like too glossy a coat to wear, but for the sake of convincing pupils to work, we can just call it 'getting better'. The better you get, the closer you are to mastery. Grit is carrying on despite the pain. Grit is being able to practise until your fingers bleed. Grit is doing it even when it's boring.

Now, I'm often suspicious of lesson time spent on ill-defined, so-called 'metacognitive skills'. But it can be profitable to teach pupils enough about the process of learning to enable them to monitor, control and regulate their own practice. We should definitely encourage them to see that hard work is its own reward and that anything worth learning will be challenging. At the explain stage of the teaching sequence, I'll begin a new topic by banging on about how hard it is; that they'll struggle but that this is normal: if it wasn't difficult what would be the point in doing it? I tell them that they will make mistakes and that not only is this OK, it's essential. I tell them that they can achieve more than they believe possible if they're prepared to put in the effort, and that whatever they *do* achieve will be exactly proportionate to that effort.

But being prepared to persevere with the gritty stuff of learning difficult concepts and mastering new skills is greatly enhanced if pupils are in possession of a growth mindset. Dr Carol Dweck contends that we all have either a fixed or a growth mindset about our abilities in particular areas.[17] For instance, whilst we might be perfectly prepared to accept that our intelligence is fixed, we might happily accept that our personalities can change and develop. Or, we might readily believe that we have the capacity to be an excellent trombonist, but despair at ever being able to solve quadratic equations. But although we're all a mix of mindsets, we tend to have a predominantly fixed or growth mindset to learning. Essentially, growth mindset folk embrace challenges, persist in the face of setbacks, see effort as the

17 Carol Dweck, *Mindset: The New Psychology of Success* (New York: Random House, 2006).

path to mastery, learn from criticism and take inspiration from the success of others. Fixed mindset bods take an opposite view; they tend to avoid challenges, give up easily, see effort as fruitless, ignore useful negative feedback and feel threatened by the success of others. As you can well imagine, a growth mindset is a jolly useful thing to possess. But what if we're feeling fixed? Is there anything we can do about it?

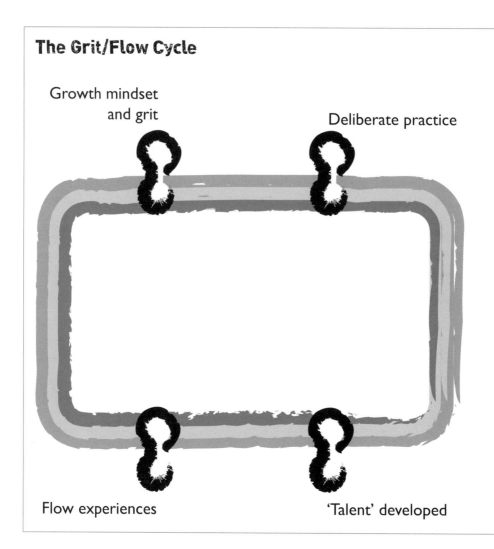

The Grit/Flow Cycle

Growth mindset
and grit

Deliberate practice

Flow experiences

'Talent' developed

Happily, there is. Just explaining the concept has an impact – pupils tend to be fascinated by the idea – and this will provide a platform for challenging fixed beliefs. It's also worth understanding the role of praise. For some people, self-esteem is so bound up in their view of their own ability that praising them for their innate intelligence can foster a fixed mindset, whereas praising effort and outcomes can help nurture a growth mindset. Habitual praising of pupils for what they *are*, rather than what they *do*, can reinforce the idea that intelligence is fixed.

Key to lines

 Resilience

 Effort

 Reflection

Grand Unified Theory of Mastery
Source: Tube map design by Pete Jones, based on ideas by Roo Stenning and David Didau.

Deliberate practice

The path to mastery depends on understanding the value of deliberate practice. 'Deliberate' practice is quite distinct from plain old vanilla practice. It involves constantly striving for improvement, carefully monitoring your performance and specifically practising the stuff you're not good at. Boring? Well, maybe not. Some kids commit many hours to playing computer games where the goal is to master the game and reach the end. They get constant and instant feedback about what works and what doesn't and then they get the opportunity to try out this feedback again and again until they get it right. Pupils who quickly throw in the towel at school are willing to persevere at *Call of Duty* until they overcome their limitations. Why do they do it? Because they want to win. Being killed endlessly is all kinds of frustrating; the pleasure comes from mastery.

But why is it that these same kids moan at doing something hard in class? What is it that 'engages' them with computer games but turns them off with, say, grammar? Well, mainly it's because choosing to squish things in your own time is fun and writing stuff in books because you're told to isn't. But fun be damned! 'Sometimes learning is not fun. Instead, it is just hard work; it is deliberate practice; it is simply doing some things many times over.'[18] If our pupils always expect 'fun' lessons they will never get good at what we're trying to teach them. But be warned: without corrective feedback on misconceptions and mistakes, practice may just be encoding failure. Most errors should have been picked up in the scaffolding phase, but we must make sure that we have sky-high expectations and clear models to refer back to.

'Talent' developed

When we start getting good at something, we start to see the point of all that practice. If we accept that talent is the product of the deliberate practice an individual has put into mastering a skill, then we can help to explode some of the 'short-cut culture' which is so prevalent in so many pupils' attitudes to school. We're much

18 John Hattie, *Visible Learning for Teachers: Maximizing Impact on Learning* (London: Routledge, 2012), p. 108.

too inclined to just see the performance of a professional athlete, musician or, dare I say it, teacher and conclude that, well, it's alright for them. They obviously have a God-given talent, and we don't. So why bother trying? What we *don't* see are the hours and hours that have gone into producing that performance. We don't see the failures, the sweat or the frustration, so we conclude it mustn't be there.

This came home to me when I was observed teaching by some newly qualified teachers seeking to develop their questioning. They watched a lesson where pupils carried out a very sophisticated, high-level discussion with very little input from me. The kids took turns at evaluating each other's responses and everyone in the class took part – it looked great. Unfortunately, the NQTs learned very little. They went away having just seen the independent construction phase of my teaching sequence and believed (wrongly) that I'm somehow a more talented teacher than they are. They hadn't seen any of the struggle or frustration that the class and I had gone through to get to this. They hadn't seen me explain, model and scaffold what I wanted. Just seeing the tip of the iceberg is not very useful for helping us understand what an iceberg looks like.

I suspect there's not a musician or sportsperson alive who will not readily 'fess up to the belief that natural 'talent' is almost irrelevant. You only get to the top of your game through determination and hard work. But when talent is developed and all the hard work seems to suddenly pay off, we're granted magical moments when everything just seems to 'flow'.

Flow experiences

The flow state is that mystical space where we become totally immersed in the experience of performing a task. If we can achieve this, the theory goes, we'll perform to a higher standard. Flow has been billed as an 'optimal experience [in which] concentration is so intense that there is no attention left over to think about anything irrelevant. Self-consciousness disappears, and the sense of time becomes distorted.' This kind of activity is 'so gratifying that people are willing to do it for its own sake, with little concern for what they will get out of it, even when it is difficult or dangerous.'[19] Sounds good, right? Maybe too good. It almost sounds addictive, doesn't it?

In our quick-fix culture, the belief that we're somehow entitled to experience flow without effort is pernicious. This is something that slavish demands to demonstrate progress every 20 minutes only exacerbate. The effortless beauty of the flow state might seem to be the antithesis of the grit needed to start on the path to mastery, but flow is the much-needed pay-off for all our effort. But it only seems to come about when we least expect it; wishing for it won't help. Delaying this gratification could well be the master skill.

But I worry about those lessons that just seem to flow. Are pupils learning or just performing really well? We're conditioned to look at the tip of the iceberg and the graceful swan above the surface. We often say that learning is messy, but do we believe it? When learning is *really* happening, short-term performance may be reduced; it feels like we're actually getting worse. Which is perhaps why we shy away from gritty where pupils grapple with difficult concepts.

But if the journey is *always* hard we may not have the motivation to carry on. We need to glimpse the magic of flow in order to trudge on and experience it again. If life was *just* rehearsal, if sport was *just* training, what would be the point? We train because we want to perform at our peak when it really matters. For our pupils this may well be in their examinations; for us it may well be in that high-stakes observation when the inspector comes to call. Whatever the reason, we want to be able to experience flow when it counts.

The role of feedback

We all know that giving feedback improves performance. And if it were as easy as that, all would be well. But, as teachers, we need to know what kinds of feedback to offer in a given situation. Sometimes a simple 'right' or 'wrong' might be enough; at other times it needs to be much more complex. For feedback to be effective it needs to meet a whole host of conditions:

---

19 Mihaly Csikszentmihalyi, *Flow: The Psychology of Optimal Experience* (New York: Harper and Row, 1990), p. 71.

- Specific – as Ron Berger says, feedback should be as specific as 'put more stripes on the legs' or 'make the tail black'. It's no good telling pupils to 'use more expression in your writing'.[20] If they knew how to do that, they'd probably already have done it.

- Clear – sometimes even specific feedback isn't clear. Make sure you are able to describe exactly what you want and use questioning to make sure that pupils understand.

- Limited – too many instructions are overwhelming. It's much more likely that pupils will improve when offered one piece of advice at a time. Consider which piece of feedback is most likely to have an impact first.

- Kind – it's all very well being kind but this also requires honesty. Berger talks about feedback needing to be 'hard on content, soft on people'. If our feedback makes people feel bad, they're not going to listen. One of the simplest ways to offer feedback that is palatable enough to hear is to phrase it in the form of a question: 'Have you considered adding more adjectives to that second sentence?'

- Balanced – this is a tough one to get right. If we only focus on correcting negatives, we can easily miss the opportunity to give feedback on what pupils are already good at. But it turns out that positive feedback can be counter-productive. Saying 'well done' might feel good but it won't help anyone improve: 'if you are not challenged you do not make mistakes. If you do not make mistakes, feedback is useless.'[21] We must ensure that the work pupils are doing is hard enough that they will make mistakes if we're going to help them improve. But we can still focus on the positive: 'Your sentence structure is really improving – now see if you can embed some subordinate clauses.'

- Timely – if our feedback is going to have impact it has to come at the right time. And the right time is usually immediately. Hard to do in a classroom situation. Waiting a week to mark books probably won't be useful but we also

---

20 Ron Berger, Ron Berger on Critique, Part 2 [video] (1 December 2012). Available at: <http://howtovideos.hightechhigh.org/video/275/Ron+Berger+on+Critique+part+2+of+2>.

21 John Hattie, quoted by Warwick Mansell in 'Pupil–Teacher Interaction', *TES* (21 November 2008). Available at: <http://www.tes.co.uk/article.aspx?storycode=6005411>.

need to have a life. The most useful feedback is therefore often verbal. But what isn't written down is easily lost and forgotten. I hate the idea of verbal feedback stamps in pupils' books – who are we doing this for? Instead, have them repeat the feedback and articulate precisely what they are going to do differently. In this way we can 'lock it in.'[22]

- Helpful – if pupils don't understand how the feedback will help them improve then it's hard to commit to acting on it. If we take the time to describe a solution which focuses on the 'so that ...', pupils are more likely to see the point: 'You should use discourse markers to connect your paragraphs together *so that* your writing is more coherent.'

Independent construction

Independence isn't possible without a period of dependence. When universities complain that undergraduates are unable work independently they assume that the reason must be too much spoon-feeding in schools. Actually the opposite is true; they aren't good at being independent because they have been made to work with too little direction and don't know how to work independently. To be independent we need to know what to do and how to do it. And if we don't teach pupils what they need to know we run the risk of them never discovering it.

The four stages of the teaching sequence are all essential components of independence. Explaining and modelling requires teachers to be experts and explicitly teach. Scaffolding allows us to start to let go and pass on the baton. As long as pupils are sufficiently clear about what they are meant to be doing then collaborative and reciprocal teaching can be highly effective. And then we need to let them practise. Practice will make permanent. If we are there to offer feedback to prevent them encoding failure, they can and will become truly independent. We need to be able to explain what we're doing and why we're doing it. Teaching should never be judged as outstanding if teachers are unclear about how their lessons fit into a sequence. We should rid ourselves of the myth that performance is evidence of

---

22 Lemov et al., *Practice Perfect*, p. 136.

learning and instead be able to say, 'Here is where they will be independent and this is how I know ...'

As teachers, it's about knowing when to apply the different skills of the teaching sequence. It's about knowing that if we expect pupils to run before they can walk we're going to have a lot of grazed knees. And it's about having the confidence to reclaim our professional expertise. We are the experts. No one else knows our pupils, in our classrooms, the way we do.

Independence vs. independent learning

As we all know, sometimes pupils need us to talk to them if they are going to have any hope of understanding new concepts and ideas. Equally, it seems to have become received wisdom that Ofsted (and school leaders) want to see independent learning and minimal teacher talk whenever they observe a lesson.

Daisy Christodoulou points out how ridiculous this is with particular reference to Ofsted's critique of a modern foreign language lesson in which Year 4 pupils were lauded for their knowledge of French spelling and being able to do things spontaneously. However, Ofsted make no reference to the methods used to teach them. Did they arrive at school with this knowledge? Did they acquire it through some sort of mystical osmotic process? We have no idea. As Daisy says, 'If it were really the case that they took spontaneously to spelling in French, why would such pupils need a school or a teacher? If, as I suspect, their ability to spell in French is actually down to teacher instruction and explanation that happened prior to the Ofsted inspection, then such descriptions are highly misleading and even dangerous.'[23]

The implication is that in good or outstanding lessons pupils will just know stuff. There should be no need for teachers to explain anything; if a teacher does explain something they are often criticised for talking too much. This insanity has led to teachers showcasing lessons that don't require pupils to know

---

23 Daisy Christodoulou, *Seven Myths about Education* [ebook] (London: The Curriculum Centre, 2013), loc. 726.

anything beyond their own life experiences. And this leads, inexorably, to setting tasks with very low expectations; stuff like writing persuasive letters to head teachers about school uniform. Teachers, especially in observed lessons, are unwilling to risk teaching pupils anything new because this would require them to speak for too long and wouldn't demonstrate pupils' ability to learn independently. If this is true, and instinctively I think we know it is, who is responsible for the 'dumbing down' schools are criticised for perpetrating?

Explaining and modelling are very difficult, if not impossible, to properly accomplish without talking. When explaining a new concept we need to be clear and precise, providing subject-specific vocabulary and structures. You could possibly use a textbook or worksheets to do this, but I doubt that Ofsted would approve of this approach any more than they would of the teacher having to talk. You can, in some circumstances, use a jigsawing approach, but to do this too often is inefficient, open to pupils' misunderstandings and would soon become dull. How much easier would it be to simply skip this step and go straight to some 'independent learning' about something your pupils already know?

And then we have the modelling and deconstruction stage of the teaching cycle. Here the teacher will explicitly show the pupils how a text works within the domain they are studying. There are lots of ways to reverse engineer texts to show how they are structured and some of these can be done independently with pupils discovering the structures for themselves. But when I trained to be a teacher, the Teaching Sequence for Writing, which involves lots of deconstruction and modelling, was considered best practice. Teacher talk used to be held up as an essential component of teaching writing and was described as 'the verbalisation of the reader and writer thought processes involved as the teacher is demonstrating, modelling and discussing'.[24] It goes without saying that verbalisation is pretty tricky without talking.

The joint construction phase is all about scaffolding language and providing pupils with enough guidance for them to attempt a task successfully. We could at this

---

24 Department for Children, Schools and Families, *The National Strategies – Primary. Talk for Writing in Practice: The Teaching Sequence for Writing*. Ref: 00467-2008PDF-EN-21 (2008). Available at: <http://www.teachfind.com/national-strategies/teaching-sequence-writing-0>.

stage just let them get on with it independently. They might, through a process of trial and error, be able get the hang of constructing an academic text. It's more likely, though, that they will revert to using everyday, non-academic language and produce a response lacking in the qualities we look for in the most able. So, the problem in doing this is one of low aspirations for our pupils. Making them practise independently before they are clear on what to do runs the risk of encoding failure. Practice does not make perfect, it makes permanent. Without sufficient instruction from an expert, pupils will get good at doing tasks badly. And who, in their right mind, wants that? That said, there's a fair bit of scope for independent learning here and Ofsted might approve of a lesson at this stage of the cycle as long as the teacher was able to conceal the guilty fact that at some stage they'd had to talk in order to explain the concept being studied, deconstruct examples and model expert processes.

Then, finally, pupils are ready to work independently. If Ofsted observe a lesson at this stage of the cycle they might expect to see the pupils working in silence and the teacher with his feet up drinking coffee. Or even better, in my classroom, they would find me working silently as well. Modelling every part of the process is important and I take care to write with my pupils at every available opportunity. This is true independence. Surely, this is what we're teaching pupils to be able to do. We want them to have the confidence and ability to complete tasks by themselves without us there to nag and prompt them. It is, however, at complete odds with the nonsense that's pedalled as 'independent learning'.

Single lesson observations are a poor way to judge a teacher's quality. If I only ever saw a teacher presiding over group work and independent learning this might be serious cause for concern. Likewise, if I only ever saw a teacher engaging in instruction from the front of the class I might worry about pupils' lack of opportunity to practise what they'd learned. Surprisingly, this whole teaching cycle is remarkably similar to the dictums of Direct Instruction as conceived by Siegfried Engelmann;[25] it's all part of the same cycle of moving pupils to being able to work independently.

....

25 Siegfried Engelmann, *Theory of Instruction: Principles and Applications* (Eugene, OR: ADI Press, 1982).

Trying to shoehorn this cycle into a single lesson robs pupils of the time they need to develop their thinking and engage in extended practice. The belief that learning is neat and takes place conveniently in 50 minute or one hour chunks is actively unhelpful. It doesn't. Teachers know this. We know, at certain stages in a topic, that we will want our pupils to do different things if they are ever going to be independent. Sometimes this will require us to talk, sometimes it won't. But to expect every lesson to show evidence of independent learning is madness. Whenever we teach or observe a lesson, we need to ask some questions:[26]

- Where does the lesson fit into a sequence? Where are the pupils along the journey to independence?

- Is this learning activity compatible with an overall process that could lead to strong outcomes?

- Is it reasonable for progress to be evident within this lesson, or might I need to see what happens over the next week or so?

- What general attitudes and dispositions are being modelled by teacher and pupils? Do they indicate positive learning-focused relationships compatible with an overall process that leads to strong outcomes?

- Does the record of work in books and folders, with the feedback dialogue alongside the work itself, tell a better story than the content of the one-off performance in front of me?

Independence is the end, not the means. If we really want our pupils to be able to use language with facility, solve complex equations and spell in French, we need to avoid the pointless horror and inherent low expectations of 'independent learning' as a means. Compelling teachers to talk less and facilitate pupils' independent learning has the unfortunate consequence of making pupils less independent. If we really want to promote pupils' independence, we need to model and explain more effectively and encourage our pupils to practise these vital and sadly neglected skills.

....

26 These questions are adapted from Tom Sherrington's blog post: Planning a Lesson Sequence; Observing a Lesson Sequence, *Headguruteacher* (16 June 2013). Available at: <http://headguruteacher.com/2013/06/16/planning-a-lesson-sequence-observing-a-lesson-sequence/>.

Chapter 3
Planning lessons for literacy

Failing to plan is planning to fail.

Smug teachers, everywhere

Planning principles

Most of this chapter is general advice on planning rather than specific advice on how to plan to include literacy in your lesson. This is for two reasons:

1. Literacy is not a bolt-on extra – it should be at the very core of your lessons. You can't 'do' literacy separately from your subject.

2. Planning is planning. I wouldn't approach the planning of one topic differently from any other.

Lesson planning can sometimes seem to suck up a disproportionate amount of time and energy. Looking back over those frenetic early years of teaching, it's become increasingly clear that I wasted an awful lot of effort designing activities rather than considering what my pupils needed to learn. That is to say, I put most of my effort into things that had only a marginal impact on learning.

The Pareto Principle, or 'the law of the vital few', suggests that in most fields of endeavour, people spend 80% of their time on those activities that produce 20%

of the impact. Or, to put it the other way, what I spend 20% of my time on will account for 80% of the impact I achieve.

What if, I started to wonder, I tried to turn those percentages around? What if I were to spend more of my time on those parts of my job that have the most impact and stop bothering with the guff? Well, in my increasingly obsessive quest for efficiency, I've arrived at the five (fairly obvious) principles below.

1. Time is precious

So, how can teachers' time be most profitably spent? Research suggests that feedback is top of the list and, for me at least, this is closely followed by absolute clarity on what, exactly, my pupils need to learn. Instead of planning individual lessons, I want to invest my time in medium-term planning to break down the skills and knowledge they will need to learn to arrive at their destination. And as for feedback, there may be all sorts of really efficient ways to give feedback during lessons, but for me, nothing beats marking their books. Sitting on a pile of unmarked work for weeks is useless, though – to have impact it needs turning around as quickly as possible. If I can set up lessons so that I'm marking whilst the pupils work then so much the better. But when that's not possible, I need to make sure that whatever time I have available is time spent marking.

2. Marking *is* planning

Pupils do work, I mark it with feedback that requires them to do (or redo) something and then they do it. Based on my knowledge of each individual I will have a good idea of what they're capable of and whether the work they've handed in demonstrates progress. Instead of just writing down feedback, I ask them individual questions, and set focused tasks for them to complete in Dedicated Improvement and Reflection Time (DIRT). I aim to mark a class's books regularly enough that at least one out of every four lessons is spent acting on feedback. Not only does this mean that every student in the class has a uniquely differentiated lesson plan, it also means that I don't have to fritter away my time planning 'activities' (see Chapter 7 for more details).

3. Focus on learning *not* activities

I consider myself the enemy of activities! Loading lessons with things to do actively gets in the way of pupils learning whatever was your clear, thoughtful objective. Time spent planning card sorts, writing worksheets and lovingly crafting resources is, by and large, time wasted. Or at least time that could have been spent doing something more profitable. It *is* worth spending time thinking about how pupils will use language in the lesson: how do they need to think, speak and write? If they're going to read, what will they need to know about the texts and what strategies can you give them to help them read more effectively?

Top tip: ask yourself, what will pupils think about during the lesson? What they think about is what they will remember.

4. Know your pupils

This sounds insultingly obvious but is easily forgotten. It's a widely accepted truism that good teaching is founded on good relationships. Good relationships are, in their turn, founded on detailed knowledge and understanding of the kids you teach. At Clevedon School we use a system called pen portraits. Every term we write a mini 'portrait' of five pupils in each class based on the data we collect and our knowledge of their personalities, backgrounds and potential. By the end of the year you will have written a portrait of every student in every class you teach. This is all fine and dandy, but what gets done with this information? I try to work out how exactly how I might be able to help these particular pupils and make sure that every student I teach gets at least one lesson (but in practice more) which has been planned just for them. And I tell them: 'Today you are my pen portrait student and this lesson is yours!'

Also, knowing your pupils makes you bulletproof! *You* are the indisputable expert on how *these* pupils learn in your classroom, and woe betide anyone who comes in shouting the odds about what *they* would do differently!

5. The 'one in four' rule

Let's be realistic, churning out Outstanding™ lessons five or six times a day, every day, is almost certainly unsustainable. Working yourself into the ground benefits no one. In any given week, I'll spend a disproportionate amount of my planning time on one or two lessons, but most will be put together in five minutes or less. My formula is that if every fourth lesson for every class is a corker, all will be well. Pupils are forgiving creatures. They will happily dine off a barnstorming lesson for a week. Plus, if a lesson is worth its salt it ought to produce work that is marked and then becomes next lesson's menu anyway.

Lesson plans

Like many teachers, I have utter contempt for planning pro formas which often descend into a pointless round of box-ticking and planning for planning's sake. This immediately falls foul of my first planning principle. Happily though, Ofsted have stated explicitly that there is no need for a written lesson plan; all they're interested in is evidence of planned lessons and tell us 'excessive detail within these plans causes teachers to lose sight of the central focus on pupils' learning'.[1]

Therefore, my lesson planning consists of considering the following five questions:[2]

---

1   Ofsted, *Moving English Forward*. Ref: 110118 (2012). Available at: <http://www.ofsted.gov.uk/resources/moving-english-forward>, p. 14.

2   Adapted from the Lesson Progress Map developed by John Tomsett at Huntingdon School, York. Available at: <http://johntomsett.files.wordpress.com/2012/06/huntington-lesson-progress-map-may-2012.docx>.

1. How will last lesson relate to *this* lesson?

All too often the skills and knowledge learned in one lesson are not revisited in the next. This assumes that if pupils have performed they must have learned. This is not the case. (See question 5 below.) If your lessons are following the teaching sequence outlined in the previous chapter, this should not be a problem.

2. Which pupils do I need to consider in *this particular* lesson?

If I know my pupils then this is a darned sight easier. (And if you write pen portraits of your pupils, it's a cinch!) Simply decide who you're going to focus on, what their particular needs are and let them know when they arrive that they're the lucky beneficiary of all your expertise and wisdom for today. Unsurprisingly, this has an enormous impact on the motivation of said student; you can practically see them glow. And really, is there any better evidence of differentiation or personalised learning? I think not.

3. What will pupils do the moment they arrive?

Lesson time is too precious to waste having pupils sitting around waiting for tardy classmates to arrive – give them some bell work that they can be getting on with as the bell goes. This can be as straightforward as putting a question on the board, but can also be used to build anticipation for the lesson ahead by projecting pictures or playing music. One of the biggest mistakes new teachers make is spending too long on bell work. Take quick feedback from one or two pupils if you must, but then move on. Never lose sight of the fourth planning question.

4. What are they learning, and what *activities* will they undertake in order to learn it?

I don't care whether you refer to them as objectives, outcomes or intentions, but you do need to have considered what it is the pupils are in your classroom to learn, and how this will help them achieve within the big picture of your medium- to long-term plan. Most planning time gets wasted on activities rather than learning. Think about the Pareto principle here and spend 80% of your time planning the objective. I've grown to love the learning outcome and, in particular, the way Zoë Elder suggests splitting it with 'so that': we're learning X so that you can do Y.[3] This then makes step 5 much clearer.

The activity is largely irrelevant. What's really important is what pupils spend the lesson *thinking* about because that's what they'll remember. So, if you want pupils to learn about, say, osmosis, it won't help for them to be asked to write rap or perform a short play. This would only distract them from the idea of osmosis and instead make them think about rapping or acting. These might well be fun and interesting activities but they will only be a distraction from what you want pupils to learn.

5. How will I (and they) know if they are making *progress*?

If you've designed your learning outcome well then it should be straightforward to check progress. If pupils have learned, then they will have produced the desired outcome.

Or will they? We should be wary of what I call the input/output myth: what we as teachers put in, pupils will, de facto, learn. Graham Nuthall talks about the mythical belief that 'engaging in learning activities (such as listening to the teacher

---

3   See Zoë Elder's blog post: Constructing Learning SO THAT It Is Meaningful and Purposeful, *Full On Learning* (1 October 2012). Available at: <http://fullonlearning.com/2012/10/01/constructing-learning-so-that-it-is-meaningful-and-purposeful/>.

talking, discussing the results of an experiment, or writing a report of an investiga-
tion) transfers the content of the activity to the mind of the student'.[4]

Sadly, this is not so, because 'as learning occurs, so does forgetting'.[5] If all this sounds
chaotic and unpredictable, that's because it is. As Dylan Wiliam has so poetically
said, 'learning is a "liminal" or "threshold" process, at the boundary between control
and chaos'.[6] It's hard enough for teachers who see pupils every day to have a handle
on their progress; someone observing for only 20 minutes will have no chance.

To make matters even more complicated, we also need to disassociate learning
from 'performance': 'Basically, current *performance*, which is something we can
observe, is an unreliable index of *learning*, which we must infer'.[7] That is to say,
performance is easy to observe whereas learning is not. You can tick a box to show
that pupils' performance has moved from X to Y but you can't always tell whether
learning has taken place. There are many instances where learning occurs but
performance in the short term doesn't improve, and there are instances where
performance improves but little learning seems to happen in the long term.

Just because pupils have been able to respond to cues doesn't mean they will have
retained what has been taught. True progress cannot take place in a single lesson
but, if everyone knows the learning destination, we ought to be able to judge how
close we are to arriving.

However, we can check whether what pupils have said and the evidence in their
books matches the expectations of our medium-term plan. If it doesn't, teach it
again. If it does, move on, but beware that what you *think* pupils have learned may
well be forgotten by the time they need it, so ensure you plan to revisit this learning multiple times.

....

4   Nuthall, The Cultural Myths and Realities of Classroom Teaching and Learning, p. 28.

5   Nuthall, The Cultural Myths and Realities of Classroom Teaching and Learning, p. 24.

6   Dylan Wiliam, Assessment, Learning and Technology: Prospects at the Periphery of Control.
    Keynote address at ALT-C, the 14th International Conference of the Association for Learning
    Technology, Nottingham, 4–6 September 2007. Available at: <www.alt.ac.uk/docs/altc2007_
    dylan_wiliam_keynote_transcript.pdf>, p. 5.

7   Robert A. Bjork, Desirable Difficulties Perspective on Learning. In H. Pashler (ed.), *Encyclopedia of
    the Mind* (Thousand Oaks, CA: Sage Reference, 2013). Available at: <http://bjorklab.psych.ucla.edu/
    pubs/RBjork_inpress.pdf>, p. 1.

Also consider how you will help pupils themselves know what progress they've made. Chapter 7 contains a range of strategies for improving feedback and assessment.

'Break' your plan

The more practised you become, the quicker you'll be able to rattle through these five questions. The only other advice I'd offer is to conduct a thought experiment in which you anticipate what might go wrong. This process of 'breaking' the plan lets you know where the weak spots might be. Knowing your pupils is crucial for this to be effective but all it involves is running though your lesson and thinking about how they will react and respond at given moments. For me it becomes like a game of chess:

> *I'll say x, and then she'll do y. OK, so I need to do …*
>
> *When I want them to do x, he'll need extra support so I need to make sure I'm free to support by doing y.*

If it's a high stakes lesson, I might spend a while doing this but normally a couple of minutes spent thinking in this way is all it takes to ensure that most of the kinks you can anticipate are ironed out.

So, these are the lessons I've learned about planning lessons. They are, of course, just my thoughts although they are underpinned by years of bitter experience.

Chapter 4
Oracy

Talk is the sea upon which all else floats.

James Britton

Oracy basics

Although there are many lessons where pupils don't have to read or write, I have yet to see a lesson in which there is no talking. If you're teaching drama, PE or any other subject in which there seems to be limited scope for demonstrating your ability to explicitly teach literacy, fear not – you can focus on speech.

Questioning

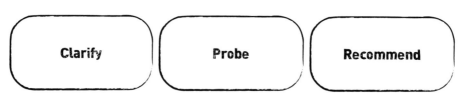

| Clarify | Probe | Recommend |

When asking questions, make it clear how they are being used to get pupils to *clarify*, *probe* and *recommend*.

I use these three question types to make it clear to pupils what type of thinking they are expected to do. If we want pupils to *clarify* their meaning we might ask something like:

- What did you mean by …?

- Can you explain that differently?

- What other words could you use?

To *probe* answers we might ask:

- Can you tell me more about …?

- What else do you know about …?

- How else might you use that?

Once they've heard a few different answers, I will ask pupils to make recommendations and ask them things like:

- What is better about …?

- Can you explain why you prefer that?

- Why do you agree with …?

Modelling

Instead of just settling for the correct spelling of subject-specific terminology, model how academic language is used in your subject area. Pupils will automatically revert to incorporating new vocabulary into everyday speech and say things like, 'When there's a big load in a river it doesn't erode as much.' But if we want to model how a geographer might use this vocabulary, we should instead get them to see how subject specialists use their specialised language and say, 'The increase in load results in a decrease in erosion.'

We need to be aware of how keywords are nominalised in subject-specific language and model to pupils exactly how to think, speak and write like subject specialists.

Prompting

Once pupils have had subject-specific speech modelled, we need to prompt them to use it. It's worth explaining that it is much easier to write something down if you have already said it. For highly literate people, transferring thoughts from everyday language to academic language is easy; for some of our pupils this will be a stumbling block. So, when a pupil offers one of those excellent suggestions which is confused in structure or marred by sloppy language use, offer them a scaffold to help them reframe their thoughts in academic language.

These scaffolds can be Thought Stems (see page 83) which can be placed around the walls of your classroom for pupils to refer to, or they can be mere rewordings, which you ask pupils to repeat so that they start to think in academic language.

What is oracy?

Pupils spend a lot of talking, don't they? Everyone can speak, so why would we want to waste valuable time teaching kids how to do it? Well, whilst this is undoubtedly true, many pupils don't speak *well*. This, I hasten to add, is not the same as being well spoken.

The concept of 'oracy' has been with us since 1965, when researcher Andrew Wilkinson coined it in an attempt to escape the woolliness of 'speaking and listening' and create parity with the more respected terms of 'literacy' and 'numeracy'.[1] Speaking and listening has long been the poor relation in the English curriculum and seems set to become increasingly marginalised. This being the case, it's perhaps no surprise that it's also often neglected across the curriculum.

American educator E. D. Hirsch Jr equates reading with listening, and speaking with writing. He says: 'If children are brought [up] to speak and understand speech well in the early years, their reading future is bright.'[2] He suggests: 'In the classroom, the teacher can and should ask children frequently to make formal prepared and unprepared presentations to the class.'[3] Could getting pupils to focus on speaking and listening be the key to improving their reading ability?

Geoff Barton urges us to get away from the idea of teaching literacy and instead to teach literacy as an integral component of teaching and learning.[4] Nowhere is this more important than in the teaching of oracy. It's impossible to fully separate the pedagogical process of using talk to teach and teaching talk. We all use talk to teach every lesson: we either do so in a way that models high standards of oracy, or we don't.

---

1   Andrew Wilkinson, The Concept of Oracy, *English in Education* 2(A2) (June 1965): pp. 3–5.

2   E. D. Hirsch Jr, *The Knowledge Deficit: Closing the Shocking Education Gap for American Children* (Boston, MA: Houghton Mifflin, 2007), p. 35.

3   Hirsch, *The Knowledge Deficit*, p. 31.

4   Barton, *Don't Call It Literacy*, p. 1.

Cambridge professor Robin Alexander sees talk as 'essential to children's thinking and learning, and to their productive engagement in classroom life',[5] and cites evidence from over 20 major international studies that make it clear that the quality of talk within classrooms raises standards. Nuff said.

This being the case, Alexander argues that we need to do some work with teachers to improve the quality of their talk before we can hope to improve the quality of pupils' talk. He identifies six distinct functions of talk (for thinking, learning, communicating, democratic engagement, teaching and assessing) and advocates strategies for developing each discretely.

Alexander argues that talk is undervalued because it is viewed as being 'primarily social' and the teaching of talk has become mainly about pupils acquiring confidence in their communication. The problem with this is that confidence is worthless unless we have something worth saying. But, 'as psychologists, neuroscientists, anthropologists and classroom researchers have long understood, the function of talk in classrooms is cognitive and cultural as well as social.'[6]

Because of this narrow understanding of speech as 'primarily social', we're often reluctant to do more than gently facilitate the development of pupils' oracy; after all, what business do we have in asserting that our speech is better than theirs? This squeamishness is endemic in our education system. Teachers pussyfoot around pupils' inability to articulate clearly or precisely in academic language out of some misguided belief that they don't want to crush their individuality.

But talk is also cognitive. The way we speak changes the way we think. And, as in any other area, if we want to improve our pupils' communication skills, we need to actively intervene and accelerate their development.

This is, of course, not without problems. In most other areas, teachers need to be merely good at teaching in order for pupils to make progress. For instance, we can use high quality texts to model the skills required to be a great writer without ever having to write ourselves. But, because of the interactive nature of talk, teachers

---

5   Robin Alexander, *Improving Oracy and Classroom Talk in English Schools: Achievements and Challenges* (Cambridge: Cambridge University Press, 2012), p. 2.

6   Alexander, *Improving Oracy and Classroom Talk*, p. 6.

need to be highly skilled speakers in order to develop the oral competence of their pupils.

One of the biggest concerns for teachers is how much time they should spend speaking in a lesson. Teachers' talk has come to be seen as an obstacle to pupils' learning and as a result there are all sorts of ideas out there for minimising teacher talk. But this rather misses the point. If we stop teachers speaking in lessons we will prevent pupils from understanding how a subject specialist models their thinking, and how speech bridges the gap to written communication. Our efforts should not be about reducing the quantity of our speech (although this might be appropriate in certain lessons) but about improving its quality.

Teachers absolutely must talk if pupils are going to learn anything worthwhile; the trick is to make that talk as efficient and instructive as possible. Whilst it's possibly true that pupils may not be actively getting on with things while you are speaking, they may well be learning far more than they would by simply engaging in well-intentioned activities.

The ability to write well depends on our ability to speak well. As teachers, we need to model speech which moves away from everyday language and towards the academic language pupils need to access our subjects. Even if you disagree that this is an important aim, we are modelling speech all the time. We don't really get a choice about it – we're either doing it badly or well. We're either providing pupils with the language toolkit to succeed in our subjects or we're not. And that being the case, why would you want to do anything badly?

Improving classroom talk – questioning

One of the best ways to improve talk in your classroom is to focus on escaping the shackles of recitation, or Initiation-Response-Evaluation (IRE) questioning: the teacher initiates a topic, the pupil responds and the teacher evaluates their answer. IRE goes like this:

> Teacher: What is the chemical symbol for oxygen?
>
> Pupil: O.
>
> Teacher: Well done.

Whilst this kind of 'guess what's in the teacher's head' questioning has its place in assessing what pupils have memorised, it's not at all useful for getting them to do more than simply recite what's been learned. Instead, we need questioning that 'requires pupils to think, not just to report someone else's thinking.'[7]

Another problem with IRE is that once the teacher has selected a victim, everyone else in the room can relax. They're safe from further interrogation until the teacher has evaluated (well done) their stooge's response.

The 'I don't know' gambit

The answer 'I don't know' is banned in this classroom

Now, pupils are often very good at snookering us with the classic, 'I don't know' gambit. The appropriate riposte is to say something along the lines of, 'I know you don't *know* – I'm asking what you *think*.' At this point we need to stand firm

....

7   Martin Nystrand, *Opening Dialogue: Understanding the Dynamics of Language and Learning in the English Classroom* (New York: Teachers College Press, 1997), p. 72.

and make sure that they *do* think. You could hover over them and stress them or you could give them some discussion time. Either way, as long as you're clear *why* you're asking the questions, and let go of the need for 'right' answers, all should be well.

If, however, the pupil you've selected to answer your carefully chosen question is in particularly truculent mood and stubbornly insists that they 'don't know', you need a strategy to deal with this. Saying 'I don't know' really means 'Leave me alone'. If you allow pupils to decide whether or not they're prepared to participate in answering questions you're already on a slippery downward slope. It's vital to assert that *you* decide whether pupils answer questions, and to make that work you need to eliminate the 'I don't know' excuse.

Here are a few suggested options:

- Ask another pupil the same question. When they answer, return to the student who 'doesn't know' and ask them the question again. Clearly they will now have an answer as they've just heard one.

- If the class won't play ball and the second pupil you ask 'doesn't know' either, you could supply an answer yourself: 'One answer could be ...' Then return to the pupil who doesn't know and ask them the question you've just answered. This lets them know, loudly and clearly, that 'I don't know' is not an acceptable response and that you will be demanding 100% participation.

- If you're in a more playful mood, try asking them what they would say if they did know the answer – you'd be amazed at how often this yields positive results.

Pose, pause, pounce, bounce

If we use the pose, pause, pounce, bounce strategy we will ensure that the quality of whole-class questioning improves dramatically and that pupils are thinking and speaking at a much higher level.

- **Pose.** Start by making sure that the questions you pose have clear and specific purposes. I find the list of verbs suggested by Bloom's Taxonomy and the like to be hopelessly confusing. Instead, question stems such as to *clarify* (what did you mean by that?), *probe* (can you tell me more about that?) and *recommend* (which answer do you think is best?) are more than adequate (see pages 70–71).

- **Pause.** Don't just pause – stop. Give everyone a chance to actually think of an answer. There are several ways to go about this beyond just waiting. You can use some old favourites like Go for Five (write five possible answers) and Think, Pair, Share (don't neglect the *think* part!) to make sure everyone has something to contribute.

- **Pounce.** What's important here is that *you* select who answers the question. I'm all for 'no hands up' but I'm less keen on lollipop sticks or other random name generators because actively choosing who answers our questions is one of the most useful skills in a teacher's armoury. Once you've made your choice don't *actually* pounce; this conjures up images of snarling lions pursuing helpless prey across the Serengeti plains. Instead, try leaning back to allow the pupil to occupy the metaphorical space and to make yourself a bit less intimidating.

- **Bounce.** And once you've got that first answer under your belt, resist the temptation to evaluate the answer yourself. If, instead, pupils are expected to evaluate their classmates' responses by bouncing questions around the class, expectations for participation are that much higher. Select another pupil to clarify the answer that's been given, to probe further into potential meanings or to recommend why a particular answer has merit.

Whole-class questioning might look a bit more like this:

> Teacher: With your partner, discuss what you know about oxygen. [suitable pause] Dan, what do you know about oxygen?
>
> Dan: O is the chemical symbol for oxygen.
>
> Teacher: Emma, is he right?
>
> Emma: Er ... yes?
>
> Teacher: What else do you know about oxygen, Emma?
>
> Emma: You breathe it.
>
> Teacher: OK, so Sam, which of those answers do you think is the most interesting?

Everyone is on their toes waiting to be asked to participate and everyone is forced to up their game. The cognitive process of thinking of answers, framing them and then making a contribution actually makes us cleverer.[8]

The Socratic method

If not quite as old as the hills, Socratic questioning has been around ever since Socrates' programme to corrupt Athenian youth ended with his execution in 399 BC.[9] It's simply a process of asking open-ended questions and then listening to the answers and asking further, relevant questions which provoke progressively deeper thought.

So what kinds of questions should we ask? This six-step process is a useful way to structure your questions:

1.   Clarify what is meant (What did you mean by ...?).

2.   Challenge assumptions (Does this mean you think ...?).

3.   Probe for evidence and reasons (How do you know ...?).

4.   Consider different viewpoints and perspectives (Why is this better than ...?).

....

8   Dylan Wiliam, *The Classroom Experiment* (BBC Two, 27/28 September 2010) [TV series].

9   The fact that Socrates was put to death for asking difficult questions really shouldn't put you off.

5. Consider implications and consequences (What would happen if …?).

6. Question the question (I think you're right/wrong because …).

Getting pupils to explore ideas using these questions will demand that they move beyond their first knee-jerk answers to a position which has been justified and thought out.

Deeper questioning

And having been through this process, here's a brilliantly useful question grid to help you plan how you're using questions as well as getting pupils to design their own:

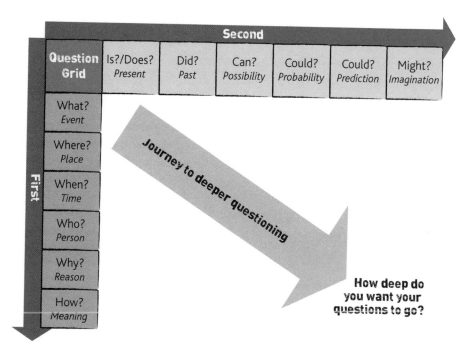

Deeper questioning grid

Source: Adapted from John Sayer's deeper questions grid: Questioning, *John Sayers Geography Blog* (6 January 2013). Available at: <http://sayersjohn.blogspot.co.uk/2013/01/questioning.html>.

But throughout this process the teacher is still required to talk, if not to engage in whole-class instruction. Our job is to help pupils organise ideas so that they can be used independently.

Question formulation technique[10]

One of my favourite methods for doing this is to use the question formulation technique. This is a way to explore what pupils know about a subject by getting them to ask rather than answer questions. The process can be broken down into the following steps:

1. Ask as many questions as you can on a given subject. The emphasis needs to be on quantity. Give a group of pupils some big sheets of paper and a pen each and make sure they know that they should all be adding their ideas.

2. Questions now need to be sorted into categories – are they open or closed? Sensible or silly? Concrete or abstract? Get pupils to produce a key and colour-code the questions.

3. Now they should select their 'best' questions. They should be asked to reflect on which would be the most useful to understand the topic they have been studying and pick one, two or three that they will investigate.

4. Having selected the best, they now need to refine their questions to make them 'better'. The deeper questioning grid (on page 79) is a great tool to help pupils refine their questions.

5. Finally, pupils are ready to answer their questions. Having engaged in the process of discussion and joint construction they will be far more able to provide thoughtful and considered answers.

---

10 Adapted from the Right Question Institute's question formulation technique. See: <http://rightquestion.org/education/>.

Questions which value listening

Even though talk is regarded as important for social development, we're often guilty of placing too much value on what pupils *say*. Whenever pupils are asked to discuss something in a group, the loudest, most confident individuals often dominate, and when teachers ask for feedback of the discussion, pupils tend to feed back what they've just said.

Shifting the emphasis is remarkably simple: just ask pupils to feed back what they've *heard* rather than what has been *said* in a discussion. The difference this can make to the quality of a discussion is immense. And it sends a clear message that listening is every bit as important as speaking.

Here's one of my favourite speaking and listening activities which can be adapted to fit any subject or topic:

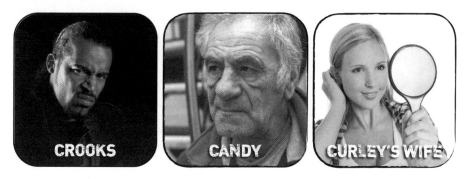

Of Mice and Men discussion: who would make the best US President?

Questioning as differentiation

It's no surprise to hear that the complexity of a question will have a bearing on the complexity of the possible answers. Teachers have been using the verbs associated with Bloom's Taxonomy to plan higher order questions since time out of mind. My preference is to use a technique called Before Before After After. Essentially, you share some sort of prompt with pupils and then ask them to describe what is happening now, what might have happened five minutes before or what might happen in 50 years.

Here's an example:

Before Before	Before	Now	After	After After

Migingo Island on Lake Victoria is claimed by both Kenya and Uganda.
The population of 131 is made up of mostly fishermen and traders

Asking what is here 'now' is relatively straightforward – all you have to do is describe what you can see. But to speculate about what was there a year before forces you to apply your knowledge of the topic, and in order to hypothesise about the future you have to imagine the consequences of overcrowding and the impact of new technologies.

Asking questions in this way allows pupils to work with content knowledge in increasingly complex ways. Task design could be as simple as deciding what questions we should ask.

If you can say it, you can write it

The other element of oracy which has important implications for how we teach is the power of generative grammar or 'talk for writing'.[11]

After much consideration, I've arrived at the following thoughts about writing:

- We can only write what we can say. Don't take this too literally – obviously we need to exclude anyone who is mute or has some sort of speech impediment. But, that aside, we are only able to put in writing that which we can express verbally.

- We can only say what we can think. It's impossible to verbalise anything which you are unable to formulate inside your head. And if you can't think in academic language that means you're not going to be able to speak in academic language either.

- But, if we can say it, we can write it.

If this is true, what does it tell us about the importance of speech?

We've all met those frustrating pupils who can verbalise fabulous ideas but as soon as they pick up a pen their mind goes blank. 'I don't know how to start!' they wail disconsolately. 'Just write down what you said a moment ago,' we urge them, but to no avail. You see, if they *could* write down what they'd said, they would have done it. The problem is that they can't. The thought processes we use for speech and writing are not the same. Try analysing spoken language some time; its garbled nature can be fascinating.

When pupils speak they often fail to consider the structure of what they're saying. Often, it isn't in sentences and they are quite literally unable to organise it into anything coherent enough to remember, let alone write down. Using Thought Stems, like the ones below, can be hugely beneficial in forcing pupils to focus on how they're speaking, not just what they're saying.

....

11 Pie Corbett and Julia Strong, *Talk for Writing across the Curriculum* (Milton Keynes: Open University Press, 2011).

Here are some examples of Thought Stems specific to English:

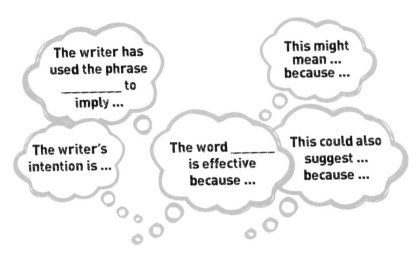

So, instead of the insipid, unfocused open questions and pointlessly meandering, conversational verbiage into which teacher-led discussion often descends, pupils are required to think using academic language. They are forced to turn the unformed maelstrom of ideas into something that has structure and, crucially, that they can remember well enough to write down.

When a pupil makes a statement or answers a question, we need to prompt them to speak like an essay, a historian or a designer. If we want pupils to 'speak like a scientist' then we need them not only to use subject-specific keywords, but we also need them to use language in a way that a scientist would. So, if we were teaching the behaviour of matter, we would, as a matter of course, introduce the keyword 'particles'. But what happens then?

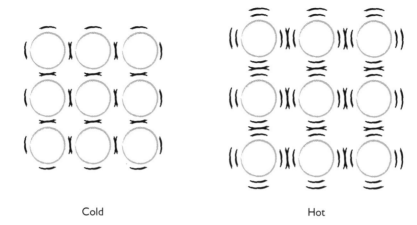

Cold   Hot

If we were to ask pupils to describe what particles were doing in different states of matter, they might say something along these lines:

> When they are cold the particles are close together, and when they are hot they move further apart.

We need to scaffold their ability to talk about this chemical reaction using scientific language. We need to show them that a scientist would be more likely to say:

> The expansion of particles causes matter to change state from solid to gas whereas the contraction of particles causes matter to change state from gas to solid.

Pupils might want to say, 'Particles in a gas are far apart', but a scientist would say, 'The particles in a gas are more diffuse.'

And because their ability to speak about states of matter has shifted, so has their ability to think. If we explicitly teach pupils to talk in this way, then they will be able to think like scientists. But we need to give them further opportunities to speak like scientists and to use their explicit language/knowledge to talk about experiments in terms of equations.

If pupils can talk about science using the language of science then they will have started to think like a scientist. And if we have changed their thinking, we will have also affected their ability to write. It should be no surprise to hear that scaffolding speech in this way leads to improved written outcomes.

By using Thought Stems to prompt pupils to reword their thoughts in the kind of language they need to use in writing, we help them not only to articulate their meaning more clearly but also, because they have practised 'speaking like an essay', they are able to write down ideas which otherwise would have remained nebulous and incomplete.

As for those 'verbally able' blighters who never seem able to capture on paper their beautiful fleeting thoughts, this insistence on 'speaking like an essay' can create a little bit of magic. I used to get so frustrated when pupils capable of uttering profound thoughts seemed unable to commit them to paper. I know now that it's not that they can't be bothered; it's that, literally, they don't have the words. If, for instance, a pupil were to say, 'When he says that thing Shakespeare is making me see that Macbeth is starting to turn evil,' we might want to provide a prompt like, 'Shakespeare has used the phrase _____ to imply ...', in order to increase the likelihood that pupils will learn to 'think like an essay' and use the academic language of your subject with the fluency and grace of young gazelles leaping from the rock of one subject to another.

The word-rich may be able to switch seamlessly between everyday and academic register with nary a pause, but not so our word-poor pupils. But modelling the process and making pupils reframe their ideas using academic language gives them the words. And, just like that, they can write it. I kid you not. We seem to have the ability to redraw our thoughts by hearing and expressing them differently. Quite simply, if we can speak it, we can write it.

Who would have believed that something so simple was so effective? Surely it should be more complicated than this? Well, of course it is. Pupils don't always enjoy being forced to respond in these ways and it takes a great deal of determination to push through the pain barrier. But if your expectations are sky-high, and you explain *why* you're doing it and persevere in the face of their pain, your efforts to model high quality talk will start to bear fruit and standards will improve.

Some other ideas for improving pupils' talk include:

- Getting pupils to work together to design their own Thought Stems using subject mark schemes to find key command words and phrases.

- Pupil-led feedback – get pupils to chair feedback and class discussions. Some pupils are naturally very good at this but the less confident could lead sessions in pairs or use prompt sheets to help scaffold their questioning.

- Paired writing – encourage pupils to discuss language and sentence choices at the point of writing.

- Listening triads – to help pupils focus on how they speak, not just what they say, get two pupils to discuss a question and the third to record their conversation. This can result in some surprising revelations for pupils.

Nominalisation – the master skill

As we've seen, it's all very well to know the key concepts and language of a particular subject but many pupils, even word-rich ones, often struggle to write with sufficient clarity and authority. The key to this is to explicitly teach pupils how to nominalise. Yeah, I know, the term 'nominalisation' is intimidating enough for teachers, let alone pupils. What the hell *is* it?

Nominalisations are efficient chunks of language that are packed full of specialist meaning. Academic language uses nouns more than verbs. For example, 'judgement' rather than 'judge', 'development' rather than 'develop', 'admiration' rather than 'admire'. If pupils can be made to see the difference between their everyday speech and the way a subject specialist thinks, speaks and writes, they are gaining access to a world in which academic success is possible and life chances are increased. And it's not only the word-poor who will benefit from being taught how to nominalise. Teaching my A level English literature class how to nominalise made an incredible impact on the quality of their essays. They could see the difference almost immediately and were rightly ashamed of the twaddle they'd been churning out previously. Learning how to nominalise is the master skill in being able to write academically.

In spoken English we usually use subjects and verbs to describe events:

> I reacted *really badly* when this bee *stung* me. My hand *ballooned* to the size of a watermelon, *turned* bright red and *started throbbing* and *itching like* crazy.

In academic language writing is much less personal and uses noun forms instead of verbs:

> Following a bee sting the normal *reaction* is *redness*, *irritation* and *itchiness* and there may be a *swelling* in the area around *the sting*.

Here are some more examples of nominalisation in action:

Everyday language	Nominalised version
Crime was increasing rapidly and the police were becoming concerned.	The rapid increase in crime was causing concern among the police.
Germany invaded Poland in 1939. This immediately caused the Second World War to break out.	Germany's invasion of Poland in 1939 was the immediate cause of the outbreak of the Second World War.
We engaged staff in the initiative by encouraging them to attend lunchtime meetings.	Staff engagement in the initiative was encouraged by attendance at lunchtime meetings.

Source: Adapted from Kerry Pulleyn's blog post: Improving the Formality of Students' Writing – Nominalisation, *The Plenary* (12 April 2013). Available at: <http://theplenary.wordpress.com/2013/04/12/34/>.

As you can see, the nominalised versions feel more expert and reliable. Basically nominalisation means using a verb (action) as a noun (concept). This is a lot simpler than it sounds and it's a great way to demonstrate to pupils how to write like subject specialists.

Let's look at some more examples of nominalisation in science:

Everyday language	Nominalised version
The amount of reactants is the same as the amount of products.	The mass of the reactants equals the mass of the products.
The equation shows the mass has stayed the same.	The equation demonstrates the conservation of mass.

It's easy to see which is preferable, isn't it?

But before you're ready to create nominalised sentences of your own, it is important to be able to identify the nominalised part of a sentence. Try reading the sentences below and identify which one contains a nominalised expression. And no cheating!

1a. The rapid increase in student numbers is causing concern at the university. More accommodation may have to be built in order to house everyone.

1b. Student numbers are increasing rapidly from year to year and the university is becoming concerned that they may need to build more accommodation in order to house everyone.

2a. The temperature of the planet is rising as a result of global warming.

2b. The rise of the planet's temperature is a result of global warming.

3a. A team of scientists analysed the data in the lab before they wrote their report.

3b. The analysis of data by a team of scientists in the lab was undertaken before writing a report.

4a. The production of a mathematical formula by mathematics and physics experts has explained the modern phenomena of network science.

4b. Mathematics and physics experts have produced a mathematical formula which explains the modern phenomena of network science.

Got it? Right, now you can check the answers below.[12]

Once you know what you're doing you start spotting nominalisations everywhere. And, more importantly, their absence becomes equally glaring. Try getting pupils to *denominalise* a text and they quickly understand why writing in this way is worthwhile.

Reasons for nominalisation

- Makes you sound like an expert (or at least someone who knows what they're on about) by making communication impersonal and authoritative.

- Makes meanings clearer.

- Adds extra information – nominalisation can count (two pints), describe (vicious attack) or classify (Alsatian dogs). You just can't do this with verbs.

- Avoids repetition – nominalisations are used to refer back to previously mentioned ideas. Nominalisations can also efficiently paraphrase what has been stated previously.

A word of caution: nominalisation doesn't make your speech better. In fact, if you go around talking like this you'll get some pretty funny looks. The advantage of using nominalisations is that it will change your thought processes and thus make it easier to write in academic language.

Improving teacher talk

As teachers we're wary of the idea of talking in lessons. Teacher talk has got itself a very bad name. But in the best examples of talk-led lessons, teacher talk is generously interspersed with questions (both to and from the teacher) and structured pupil talking.

....

12 Sentences 1a, 2b, 3b and 4a contain the nominalisations.

Back in 2008, an Ofsted inspector told me that I talked too much. I'd come to think of myself as being a pretty darned good teacher and was devastated to be told my lesson was 'satisfactory to good'. My attempts to probe this judgement got little further; he offered no criticism of what I'd said or how I'd said it, just that I'd spoken for too long.

This came as a huge blow to my self-confidence and I spent the next few years reinventing myself as a trendy, progressive teacher. Out with modelling and whole-class instruction; in with group work, problem solving and PLTS. It worked. Lesson observations were given the thumbs up and the kids were thoroughly engaged and having a great time. Smiles all round. Occasionally, some of the more academic pupils complained that they wanted me to 'just tell them stuff', but I dismissed that as the product of too much spoon-feeding from other, less exciting teachers.

But, more recently, I've come to see that Direct Instruction is a very effective way to teach and, for all the trendy arguments to the contrary, discovery learning is not. For those who may not be entirely clear, Direct Instruction can be summarised thus:

> The teacher decides the learning intentions and success criteria, makes them transparent to the students, demonstrates them by modelling, evaluates if they understand what they have been told by checking for understanding, and re-telling them what they have told by tying it all together with closure.[13]

Sounds eminently reasonable, doesn't it?

Discovery learning, on the other hand, requires the only expert in the room (you) to keep their trap shut and allow pupils to muddle through without the benefit of being told what's right and wrong. This is clearly daft and results in pupils' working memories being overloaded with too much new information. Before anyone starts frothing at the mouth with righteous indignation, let me add that there are, of course, times when we can be effective as facilitators, but these will tend to be in the scaffolding and practising stages of the teaching sequence.

---

13 Hattie, *Visible Learning*, p. 206.

Now, I'm not completely recanting – I still believe pupils need to be given opportunities to work collaboratively and to experiment with different ideas – but I'm a lot clearer on *why* I might want them to do it. I'm firmly convinced of the need to teach pupils a curriculum predicated on expanding their horizons and giving them powerful knowledge of the world beyond the sometimes narrow confines of their lives.

But perhaps the biggest shift in my thinking is on the troublesome topic of teacher talk. You see, when that inspector told me I talked too much he was basing that judgement on a body of thinking which had identified that much of what teachers were saying was guff. Teachers had had carte blanche to bang on in whatever tedious manner they decided was appropriate for far too long. It was right and proper that this view should be challenged. In his wonderfully erudite book, *Trivium 21c*, Martin Robinson points out that boring and repetitive teaching has a long and inglorious tradition stemming from 'the one way catechism (literally "to sound into ears") by which the master instructed his pupil'.[14] But it isn't the 'sounding into ears' that is boring and repetitive, it's how we go about it. Effective teachers explain well in short bursts. Ineffective teachers take longer to explain less well. This is important, as studies show that pupils' attention begins to fall off after about 10 minutes.[15]

But, predictably, as soon as it became acceptable to critique how long teachers talk, ill-informed idiots began to interpret this as a preference for teachers not talking at all. This move to reduce teacher talk has hamstrung us professionally and cut off what can be a hugely effective delivery system for all kinds of rich and interesting knowledge. No one's advocating long, boring lectures to drooling, slack-jawed pupils. Effective teacher talk is an interactive, two-way process that seeks to actively involve pupils in learning.

So, in the spirit of improving teacher talk, here are some very simple ideas you could use with pupils.

....

14 Martin Robinson, *Trivium 21c: Preparing Young People for the Future with Lessons from the Past* (Carmarthen: Crown House Publishing, 2013).

15 John Hattie and Gregory Yates, *Visible Learning and the Science of How We Learn* (London: Routledge, 2013), p. 48.

Daniel Willingham tells us: 'The human mind seems exquisitely tuned to understand and remember stories.'[16] Maybe we could improve our talk by seeking to improve our ability as rhetoricians. To this end, Martin Robinson outlines 'the five parts of rhetoric' as used in Ancient Greek education:

1. **Invention**

   Firstly you think about the content which you intend to teach and you draw together your 'evidence'. Then you establish your *Ethos*, your credibility, not your street cred but why you are a suitable person to teach this particular content (this is probably part of an ongoing dialogue where you communicate about why the subject you teach is important). Next you think about how to create the right mood, the shared emotion or *Pathos* between you and the class. You should pay particular attention to creating the right emotional charge at certain points in the lesson. Finally *Logos*, which is your use of reasoning and logic, and models critical thinking.

2. **Arrangement**

   The order in which you present your talk. For this the basic six parts of oratory are useful. 1. The *Exordium* or 'hook': something that catches the class's attention but is also central to your narrative. 2. *Prothesis*: you present the history of what you are talking about. 3. *Partitio* or division: you make the points which are uncontroversial and then the points which are contested. 4. *Confirmatio* or proof: you state your thinking. 5. *Confutatio* or refutation: you refute any opposing argument. 6. *Peroration*: you sum up the arguments and leave an impression with your class about why the content matters and why it should matter to them.

3. **Style**

   Low, medium or grand? Low style is 'down with the kids', use sparingly. Medium is probably the best for day to day teaching, but every now and then it might be good to unleash the 'grand style' of great oratory to lift the class to a higher level.

4. **Memory**

   If your talk is drawn from your *natural* memory, rather than always reading from a textbook, your credibility is enhanced. If you use PowerPoint it should be your tool rather than you being its slave. Anything on your whiteboard should illustrate and not lead your talk. NB: *Natural* memory, which is 'knowing your stuff', is better than *artificial* memory, which is more like an actor remembering a speech.

---

16 Willingham, *Why Don't Students Like School?*, p. 51.

5. **Delivery**

   Voice, gesture, posture, use of space. Without these performance skills being used to the full, the most brilliantly thought through examples of teacher talk can fall flat.[17]

Maybe by thinking in this way, we could make teacher talk something enthralling, memorable and highly engaging for pupils – all without resorting to sticky notes and sugar paper.

The power of language

Another aspect we could usefully consider in seeking to improve our teaching is the minutiae of the language we routinely use and the effects it might have.

Conjunctions: 'and' not 'but'

Whenever we say 'but' when giving instructions we're acknowledging a problem or a difficulty. We're tacitly accepting that pupils won't want to do whatever it is we want them to do:

Yes, I know quadratic equations are boring, *but* you need to understand them if you're going to pass your GCSE.

I realise you're finding this hard *but* it's really important to try your best.

What do these kinds of statements communicate? Obviously, kids are unlikely to take the time to consciously unpick your language but on an unconscious level they might hear that you're giving them an excuse not to comply. Instead we could tweak what we say by using 'and' not 'but':

I know you think quadratic equations are boring, *and* that's why I'm so impressed with your determination to master them.

I realise you're finding this hard *and* that's why it's worth doing.

---

17 Martin Robinson, Teacher Talk: Sounding Into Ears, *Surreal Anarchy* (26 October 2013). Available at: <http://martinrobborobinson.wordpress.com/2013/10/26/teacher-talk-sounding-into-ears/>

Of course, you could just change the second half of the sentence and keep the 'but'; however, making it into 'and' means that instead of creating a clash, the first clause justifies and upholds the second clause. We want to foster a growth mind-set and for pupils to have the tenacity to cope with gritty learning. Using 'and' rather than 'but' when giving instructions is small potatoes, but maybe it could help focus pupils on the benefits rather than the drawbacks of making an effort.

Personal pronouns

Could something as seemingly innocuous as a pronoun have an impact on the quality of teacher talk? Well, maybe. The following suggestions are all tiny tweaks we could easily make to our efforts to model better communication.[18]

- **First-person singular**

  'I' is the only person we can speak of with any degree of authority. Referring to anything else risks inaccuracy, arrogance or both. Saying 'I find this works' is incontrovertible whereas to claim 'this works' is problematic; saying 'You should do this' even more so. When discussing behaviour with pupils, saying 'I saw you doing this' prevents a tedious argument as to what else may have been going on and avoids discussion of motives or impact. Pupils are free to share my feelings, disagree with them or move on.

- **Third-person singular**

  My dad always used to get upset when I referred to my mother as 'she'. 'Who's she?' he'd ask. 'The cat's mother?' When we label others as 'he' or 'she' it is easier to dwell on resentments and unkindness. It's worth prompting pupils to avoid using the third-person singular. When I hear 'He keeps annoying me', our response might be to ask 'Who's he?' Somehow, 'Jake keeps annoying

---

18 Adapted from Harry Fletcher-Wood's blog post: Richard Hogarth: A Misunderstood Genius? Using Language Effectively as a Teacher..., *Improving Teaching* (15 September 2013). Available at: <http://improvingteaching.co.uk/2013/09/15/ richard-hogarth-a-misunderstood-genius-using-language-effectively-as-a-teacher/>.

me' is more useful and humanising and, on a practical note, more likely to resolve differences.

- **First-person plural**

  Using 'us' and 'we' when talking to a class is inclusive and can be a powerful way of expressing collective will. When discussing pupils' achievements, or a class's struggles, it can be really helpful to say, 'We've worked really hard on this'. It shows that you, the teacher, are part of the struggle and that you share the highs and lows of your pupils' experience.

Paying attention to these 'little bits' of language can make a difference to the way we talk and pupils listen.

Chapter 5
Reading

To learn to read is to light a fire; every syllable that is spelled out is a spark.

Victor Hugo

Reading basics

Too often in lessons pupils are asked to read textbooks or worksheets with no explicit instructions on how to go about extracting information from them. Having been in lots of lessons where this has happened, I can tell you how pupils react. Some pupils just get it. If you ask them if they know what to do they sneer at you contemptuously – of course they do. If you were to ask how they know they'd be stumped, but as they're obviously capable, why worry? But some pupils will just be stumped. They will create all sorts of excuses to explain why they're not doing the work (mainly they'll moan that it's boring), but the truth is that they aren't able to do what we can implicitly do. They see a page of text and they freeze up with that same anxiety I felt when confronted with algebra.

So, here are three basic skills that any teacher can explicitly teach whenever they expect pupils to do any reading.

1. Skimming – the ability to get a broad overview of what a text is about as quickly as possible

Consider this passage:

> The Laki eruption was one of the most devastating eruptions in human history. Iceland lies on the mid-Atlantic ridge and its volcanoes pose a constant threat, although very few of them produce violent eruptions because the magma is usually basaltic and relatively free-flowing. In 1783–84, a major eruption from the Laki fissure poured out an estimated 14 km^3 of basaltic lava and clouds of poisonous compounds. The volcano is located in a remote part of Iceland and no one was killed by the event itself. However, the secondary effects were devastating because the poisonous cloud killed over half of Iceland's livestock population, leading to a famine which killed approximately a quarter of the population. At that time, there was no system of international relief in Iceland. The dust cloud (which was much larger than that caused by the eruption of Mount Pinatubo) is thought to have reduced temperatures in Europe for several years, causing poor summers, reduced harvests and, as a result, social unrest. Some historians believe that it helped trigger the French Revolution in 1789.[1]

Expert readers will automatically have 'read' that passage and understood what it was about in seconds. Some pupils will work out very quickly whether this passage is likely to contain helpful information, others will not. The word-poor will often just see a block of text and experience an overwhelming sense of anxiety. How, they think, am I ever going to read all that? But, of course, they don't think that at all – they just shut down in order to avoid feeling stupid.

To explicitly teach skimming we can share the following information:

- The first sentence of a paragraph is often the 'topic sentence'. This sentence tells you what the rest of the paragraph will contain. If you just read the first sentence you will usually have enough information to make an accurate judgement on what the paragraph is about.

- Only certain words contain meaning. Don't bother trying to decode the little words, just focus on those words which give you information: *The Laki eruption was one of the most devastating eruptions in human history.*

....

1   David Flint, Lindsay Frost, Simon Oakes, et al., *Edexcel GCSE Geography B: Evolving Planet Student Book* (Harlow: Pearson Education, 2009), p. 21.

2. Scanning – the ability to pick out key information from a text

Have a look at this extract:

> Six kings ruled six Irish provinces, each of which had many tribes with their own kings. Traditionally a High King of Ireland claimed tribute from the other kings. The last High King was Brian Boru, King of Munster, who died in 1014 while defeating the Danes at Clontarf. His rival, the King of Leinster, aided by the Danes who, after 1014, ruled Dublin, Waterford and Limerick. Four Kings – of Leinster, Munster, Connaught and Ulster – fought for Boru's crown.
>
> In 1154 Henry II persuaded Pope Adrian IV to give him authority to conquer Ireland. In 1166 he had his chance. MacMurrough (Leinster) had stolen the wife of O'Rourke of Breffney, a neighbour of O'Connor (Connaught). All the kings condemned Mac-Murrough and banished him. He asked for Henry's help. He sent de Clare (Strongbow), Earl of Pembroke to lead an army of chain-clad knights, supported by Welsh archers. The unarmoured Irish, with their Danish battle-axes were no match for them. The English took Wexford, Waterford and Dublin.[2]

How would pupils work out how to answer the following questions?

1.   How many Irish provinces were there?

2.   When did Henry persuade the Pope to give him authority to conquer Ireland?

3.   Which cities did the English take?

Firstly, we can teach them to look for key phrases from the question in the text, that dates are made up of numbers which really stand out and that names of cities (and all other proper nouns) will begin with capital letters and are thus easy to scan for.

But it's also a revealing insight into teachers' minds that the answer to the first question is at the beginning, the answer to the second question is in the middle and the answer to the last question is at the end of the passage. Some pupils seem to instinctively understand this and others don't. If we teach them where to scan

----

2   Peter Lane and Christopher Lane, *History: Key Stage 3 Study Guides* (London: Letts Educational, 1992), p. 40.

for information we will not only be giving them explicit advice on reading, we will also help them to understand how comprehension tests work.

3. Zooming – to be able to focus on the meanings of individual words and phrases and their relevance to a text

Skimming and scanning will only take you so far. There are often times when we need to think more deeply about the information we locate in a text. I used to really struggle to explain to pupils how to analyse and evaluate the information that they pick out – my definitions were too abstract and slippery; they just couldn't remember what to do.

Like many other teachers, I've used lots of variants of the PEE paragraph to help structure pupils' attempts to analyse information. This may be useful if you already understand how to analyse information but less so if you don't. Very often, pupils simply follow the structure without actually analysing or evaluating anything meaningful.

Instead, try using a technique I call 'zooming in and out'. In brief, the skill of analysing is compared to a close-up shot in which you are able to see details you might otherwise miss, and evaluating is compared to a wide-angle shot where you can see how the details fit into the big picture.

Although I developed this technique to be useful when analysing literary texts, I've found, in discussion with teachers of other subjects, that the analogy is equally helpful in science, history, geography and so on. When we read a text, normally we just see the tree. Zooming in allows us to focus on details we'd otherwise skip over – patterns in the bark and the colour of the moss. And zooming out helps us see that the tree does not exist in isolation. It's part of a forest.

Extreme close-up

- Zooming in allows you to examine tiny details you might miss and discuss how writers use techniques
- Zoom in to focus on single words or short phrases

Wide shot

- Zooming out allows you to see the 'big picture' and discuss how the writers' techniques help us to understand their intentions
- Zoom out to focus on the whole text (or texts)

Zooming in and out

But enough metaphor, here's another text to consider:

> The food that enters the small intestine is highly acidic and here it is mixed with alkaline juices from the liver and the pancreas. This neutralises the acid and makes the pH of the small intestine slightly alkaline. About pH 8. Here the food is finally broken down into substances that are small enough to pass through the wall of the intestine into the blood where they can be transported to all parts of the body.
>
> The small intestine is well adapted for absorption. The inside is folded and the folds are covered in small finger-like projections called *villi* (one *villus*). The villi are very thin and have a large surface area. Each villus has many small blood vessels, capillaries, to carry away absorbed sugars, amino acids, water, minerals and water soluble vitamins like vitamin C. Once the food molecules have been absorbed and transported in the blood, they enter cells where they are used to make new cells and repair the body.[3]

If we 'zoom in' on the phrase 'small finger-like projections' we can analyse what villi might be like; however, we might start getting the qualities of fingers and villi confused so it's important to 'zoom out' to evaluate the phrase in light of the big picture of the text.

Depending on the complexity of the text, we might want to zoom out further to see what might be revealed about the context in which this was written. For instance, historians may want to zoom out to assess the validity and bias of the source material, and, in English, zooming out can help us establish what a writer might have wanted readers to think or feel.

Armed with these reading basics, pupils are equipped to access texts in ways that might previously have been barred to them. However, these kinds of reading skills take us only so far. Sometimes, no matter how skilled a reader you are, you'll be unable to understand a text because you simply have no idea what it's on about. The only solution to this thorny problem is to teach the background knowledge that writers assume their readers possess.

---

3   Richard Fosbery and Jean McLean, *Heinemann Coordinated Science: Higher Biology Student Book* (Portsmouth, NH: Heinemann Educational Secondary Division, 1996), p. 23.

How should we teach reading?

Reading is complex and unnatural. Our brains are designed to use and understand oral language but learning to read demands that we use 'brain areas that have evolved for other purposes such as language, vision, and attention.'[4] The ability to read is not innate and requires systematic and explicit teaching but, once learned, quickly becomes something that the word-rich take for granted. We forget the struggle and this makes it hard to empathise with the word-poor and those who get labelled as having 'reading difficulties'. In order to be a skilled reader we need to master both word recognition and language comprehension.

Word recognition is comprised of:

- Phonological awareness (recognising chunks of words – the syllables and phonemes from which words are constructed).

- Decoding (the process of turning symbols into sounds – generally taught using synthetic phonics).

- Sight recognition of familiar words.

Language comprehension breaks down as follows:

- Background knowledge (the facts or concepts referred to in a text which writers assume readers will know).

- Vocabulary (knowledge of the words used in a text).

- Language structures (understanding of syntax, semantics, etc.).

- Verbal reasoning (recognising and understanding inferences, metaphors, etc.).

- Genre knowledge (understanding of print and genre conventions – see Appendix 3).

---

4   Elizabeth Norton and Maryanne Wolf, Rapid Automatized Naming (RAN) and Reading Fluency: Implications for Understanding and Treatment of Reading Disabilities, *Annual Review of Psychology* 63 (2012): 427–452, at p. 429.

As readers become increasingly skilled, language comprehension becomes more strategic and word recognition becomes more automatic. In other words, we think less about the words and more about the meaning.[5] Our eyes will focus, briefly, on every word we read, but word-rich readers implicitly know to skip over grammatical words that don't contain meaning. Normally, we read at about 300 words per minute.[6] Any unfamiliar words slow us down as we decode them and puzzle out their likely meaning. If there are too many unfamiliar words, reading slows to the point at which it becomes increasingly difficult to comprehend a text as our brains struggle to hold unconnected meanings in overloaded working memory. If your reading speed is less than 60 words per minute, comprehension is practically impossible.[7]

So, how exactly should we teach children to read? This vexing question is uppermost in many teachers' minds. In the Early Years, we concentrate on word recognition; as this becomes increasingly automatic, pupils have sufficient working memory to concentrate on making meaning. Although we expect pupils to understand the texts we place in front of them, we put very little effort into teaching them about the genres of texts or the knowledge of language structures they might need to make sense of what they're reading. If we think about it at all, we just kinda hope they'll 'get it'.

Arguably, the reason that attempts to raise the standards of reading in schools have failed is because they've focused on teaching transferable reading skills rather than on giving pupils the background knowledge necessary to understand a wide range of texts. E. D. Hirsch Jr argues that if we want to improve reading we need to teach knowledge, and specifically, knowledge about language. Much of our thinking about education and children's development stems from Romanticism. The Romantics believed that education should be 'natural' and that pupils should be allowed to 'grow'. These words have since become synonymous with 'good'. The problem comes from the belief that children will become better at say, reading, if they are allowed to develop naturally. After all, they learn to speak without much

---

5   See Hollis S. Scarborough, Connecting Early Language and Literacy to Later Reading (Dis)Abilities: Evidence, Theory, and Practice. In Susan B. Neuman and David K. Dickinson (eds), *Handbook of Early Literacy Research*, Volume 1 (New York: Guilford Press, 2001), p. 98.

6   Hattie and Yates, *Visible Learning and the Science of How We Learn*, p. 54.

7   Hattie and Yates, *Visible Learning and the Science of How We Learn*, p. 56.

interference, don't they? Well, yes they do. But reading is a deeply unnatural thing to do; there is very little chance that a child will learn to read without help.

Here's an example of how a lack of knowledge can inhibit your ability to decode. The initial quote is from Kant's *Critique of Pure Reason* (§21):

> A manifold, contained in an intuition, which I call mine, is represented by means of the synthesis of the understanding, as belonging to the necessary unity of self-conscious-ness; and this is effected by means of the category.
>
> What are the main ideas of this passage?
>
> 1. Without a manifold, one cannot call an intuition 'mine'.
>
> 2. Intuition must precede understanding.
>
> 3. Intuition must occur through a category.
>
> 4. Self-consciousness is necessary to understanding.[8]

See the point? Comprehension depends on constructing a mental model that makes the elements fall into place and, equally importantly, enables the listener or reader to supply essential information that is not explicitly stated. In language use, there is always a great deal that is left unsaid and must be inferred. This means that communication depends on both writer and reader sharing a basis of unspoken knowledge. And what we already know is the most important indication of whether we will be able to decipher a text meaningfully.

We can't begin to form analytical interpretations until we have a decent understanding of the text. But if pupils are to get this kind of understanding they need to be taught the background knowledge of whatever topic they're learning about. Everything we read depends on knowledge, but as word-rich teachers we often take for granted what our pupils will know.

For example:

---

8   Dylan Wiliam, Principles of Curriculum Design. Presentation delivered at the SSAT Conference on Principled Curriculum Design: Tools for Schools, Manchester, 8 March 2013. Available at: <http://www.redesigningschooling.org.uk/wp-content/uploads/2012/11/Dylan-Curriculum-Presentation.pdf>, p. 19.

[W]e know that the letters t i o and n together make the sound 'tion'. We know how to pronounce that sound when we read it. We also know when and how to apply that sound and its equivalent sequence of letters to a word. Many students lack these basic decoding skills, because they lack knowledge we take for granted.[9]

So, by teaching relevant content knowledge explicitly, we will not only help pupils with their understanding of whatever text we want them to read, we'll also help build up their wider knowledge base. This, in turn, will allow them to use this knowledge in other settings.

So, back to my list of what we need to teach:

1. Decoding – we've become pretty good at this (or at least, primary teachers have). As long as kids pick this up in Year 1 or 2, they'll be fine. Problems arise if they arrive at secondary school without being able to do this well, as most secondary-trained English teachers lack the training or time to do much about it.

2. Understanding – Hirsch's claims that 'There is every scientific reason to predict that an intensive and well-focused effort to enhance language and knowledge … will not only raise reading achievement for all, it will help to narrow the gap between social groups.'[10] Bold words. And when you consider that we need to understand at least 90% of the vocabulary in a text before we can process it,[11] let alone enjoy it, then maybe expanding pupils' background knowledge doesn't seem so daft. But how can we, as classroom teachers, hope to teach all the knowledge that pupils will need to read fluently? We can't. We can, however, concentrate on teaching the vocabulary pupils will need to access the subjects we teach (see pages 170–172).

---

9   Joe Kirby, *How to Start on Teach First: English* [Kindle edn] (London: Teach First), loc. 426.

10 Hirsh, *The Knowledge Deficit*, p. 22.

11 Hattie, *Visible Learning for Teachers*, p. 51.

3. Enjoyment – the idea of more speaking and listening as the solution to improving reading and writing certainly sounds fun. But will it inspire a love of literature? This is something that teachers still need to pour their hearts and souls into, and we need to make sure that we're exposing our pupils to as broad a range of wonderful books as we can in the hope that maybe, just maybe, they'll like one of them.

Of these three areas, most teachers will only have to worry about understanding. We assume (often wrongly) that kids arrive at secondary school able to decode. The vast majority can, to a greater or lesser extent, but there will always be those who will struggle with their ability to turn the squiggles on a page into something that contains meaning. Some of these pupils will have been labelled 'dyslexic' and that may or may not help them access the subjects they will be forced to learn. But that's a topic for a whole other book. As long as your pupils comprehend what they read in your lessons, any concerns about whether they enjoy it tend to come a distant second.

So, armed with the reading basics covered in Chapter 2, most teachers will have enough information to make sure that no one is completely floundering. The balance you will need to find is between teaching your subject and teaching the background knowledge needed to access the assumptions that writers of text-books will make about what your pupils know and what they don't. Happily, to find this balance you merely need to make explicit the link between the subject knowledge you're teaching and the subject-specific language needed to make sense of the texts they will read.

But, despite Hirsch's disparaging of generic reading skills, it is worth being able to share with your pupils a taxonomy of reading skills. Here's a little something I came up with earlier:

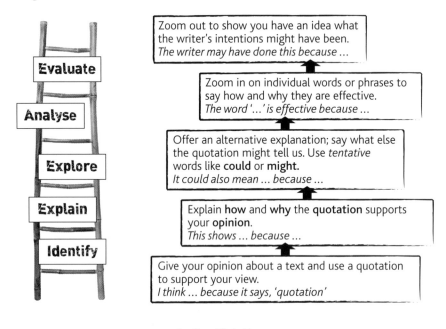

Reading skills ladder

This reading skills ladder was developed specifically for English, but teachers of other subjects have reported that their pupils have found it useful to gauge the sophistication with which they read all sorts of texts.

Guided reading

All pupils can benefit from having an expert reader model and scaffold their attempts to understand texts. Ideally, we could coach all pupils by reading with them individually. This is unrealistic, so we don't. The very weakest get one-to-one support and everybody else makes do. Back in the late 1990s, guided reading was all the rage. In essence, this simply meant dividing a class into groups of roughly equal reading ability and working with each group in turn. Whilst you are reading with one group, the others need to be getting on with answering comprehension questions or some other activity by themselves. Your role, as the name 'guided reading' suggests, is to guide the group you're working with; asking them questions, discussing possible meanings and informing them about difficult vocabulary.

The downside is that the group you're guiding soak up all your attention and everyone else needs to be trusted to get on with it. When I first attempted guided reading as a newish teacher in a school which had just failed an Ofsted inspection, my main concern was behaviour management. If, I mused, I'm supposed to be working with a small group what the hell are the rest of the class going to get up to? This is a real and important concern. If you know that pupils' behaviour is an issue, then it's important to crack that before trying something which could, potentially, end in chaos. But then that's true of almost anything we do as teachers. Pupils can't learn until order has been established and certain standards of behaviour are being met.

I'm aware that lots of primary teachers use guided reading (and writing) routinely, and that lots of English teachers implicitly teach using the reading strategies which accompany guided reading in an ad hoc way. To them, none of this will sound like any great shakes but, as far as I'm aware, this is not how texts are read across the curriculum in secondary schools.

The reading strategies are:

- Skimming

- Scanning

- Close reading (zooming)

- Questioning

- Visualising

- Empathising

- Reading backwards and forwards

- Predicting

- Inferring

We've already encountered the first three: skimming, scanning and zooming (pages 98–102), and these are the strategies I use most often and consider most important. But the others are also worth your consideration.

Questioning

As the strategy suggests, this is about developing pupils' ability to ask questions about a text to improve their understanding of it. When used with fiction, questioning is meant to get readers into the mind of the writer and start considering why certain choices have been made. But for the types of non-fiction texts used across the curriculum, these questions could be about vocabulary (what does this word mean?) or about why certain details have been included. For groups that are meant to be reading independently, you could perhaps ask pupils to identify a set number of questions they would like answered and then to answer each other's questions.

Visualising

You create a picture in your mind using the words in the text to improve your understanding. Again, this might be more useful when exploring fiction, especially when we encounter descriptive passages or interesting imagery. As an English teacher, it's a useful technique for getting pupils to think about the effects of language, but I'm not sure if there's a place for it across the curriculum.

Empathising

Being able to put yourself in someone else's shoes and feel what they feel can be extraordinarily useful in all sorts of areas. In fact, I'd go so far as to say that empathy is one of the most important life skills there is. That said, there's possibly not much call for it when exploring a science textbook.

Reading backwards and forwards

Sometimes you have to read back in a text or read forward in order to make connections to improve your understanding. This is little more than flicking back to confirm what you thought you knew based on what you have just discovered. When reading a long text, like a novel, this can be a fairly lengthy process, but usually it's just a case of skipping back and forth and combines well with skimming and scanning.

Predicting

This is about being able to make informed guesses about the text. Expert readers do this all the time and will also often combine it with skimming and scanning; we make guesses based on the information we've uncovered, and, if we know enough about the subject being discussed, these guesses will generally be accurate.

Inferring

Inferring (and its close cousin deducing) is the art of using clues in the text to work out meanings. It's about being able to work out the subtext or the implied meaning that lies beneath the surface. As such, inferring is part of the process of zooming in and out.

A word of caution: these strategies are all very well, and certainly worth explicitly sharing with pupils. But they are no substitute for possessing the background knowledge required to access whatever it is you're reading. If guided reading is to be useful, it should include a healthy dose of building the field and setting the context of the subject about which you're reading.

Analysis

If we want pupils to be more analytical (and of course we do) then we need to teach them explicitly how to do this.

Deep reading

There are loads of things we can do to help pupils read in lessons. We can break down texts, use different reading strategies, select texts that are suitable and explore unfamiliar words and their meanings. We can explore the subtext, the writer's purpose and how readers respond, but decoding – the simple reading of words and linking them together to work out the basic units of sense – is something secondary teachers shy away from. Why? Because, if you're anything like me, you assume that they have understood it. And this is what we need to address: our assumptions.

We assume too much about how pupils read. We assume the words they'll know and those they won't. We assume the speed at which they read. We assume how they will understand things. We assume that they have a certain level of proficiency in reading, yet we have nothing concrete or explicit on which to base these assumptions. More often than not, it boils down to 'they're a level 5, so they *must* be able to do it'.

This mismatch between our assumptions and reality can often be jarring. Whenever a pupil fails to recognise a word or concept, which seems so familiar to us, it can be alarming. You might be talking to Year 10 about a court of law and then a pupil asks: 'What's a trial?' How, you may very well wonder, can this pupil watch endless episodes of *EastEnders* and not understand what a trial is? But it happens.

So, what if we returned to the kind of one-to-one reading that happens in primary school? English teacher Chris Curtis did just this with his class of Year 9 pupils over several months and he made some surprising discoveries.

I sat with a pupil and got them to read to me an extract from a story. They read a photocopy and I annotated another photocopy where they struggled, broke down words or hesitated. Some were really good and read flawlessly. Some struggled. Some, who I thought would be good, struggled too. It revealed a lot about my assumptions. If they demonstrated understanding at a high level in their writing about a text, then they clearly understood the text and everything in it. In fact, that can be far from the case. One extract I read with the pupils had the word 'agony' in it. A very high number of pupils struggled to read it out correctly. So, what would they normally do in a class? They would have a strategy to cope. In fact, most of our reading teaching focuses on strategies of how to cope with difficult texts. But do these strategies fix or mask a problem?

… For some of our pupils, reading is like my journey to school. They have several traffic lights that stop the flow of thought, ideas and understanding. These traffic lights are words that they are unfamiliar with when written down. They also have to face a cyclist on the road. These cyclists are usually those long multi-clause sentences that they have to take extra care with to understand. They have to face a tractor that just stops the journey dead. The tractor is one of those words or phrases that without its meaning you can't get any further. Take the phrase 'déjà vu'.

The sudden feeling of déjà vu made Tom's stomach lurch.

Without a teacher to explain it or access to a dictionary, a pupil will not work out the meaning of this sentence, unless they know it, of course. Is it a disease? Is it an emotion? The strategies that we usually employ don't work in this case.

You could argue that the gist of a text is important, but that isn't the case when you look at exam papers and textbooks. Complete understanding is needed for some of the simplest of questions. If pupils are finding a tractor in every sentence, then their overall understanding is reduced completely. What can we do about it?

We need to work harder to avoid superficial reading in lessons. Most of the pupils I read with read quickly and that is generally fine for most, because they get the overall gist and understand the key parts of the text and then that helps them when they read for questioning. However, some pupils don't get the initial gist of a text because of these stumbling blocks. They get a picture with the key parts missing. Then, when they approach the questions they struggle as the key pieces are missing.

So, if reading a book could be said to resemble a journey, what are the things which might slow us down or present obstacles?

Traffic lights

These are the words that they might know and use verbally, but they might struggle to read them.

- Before reading a text, pick the polysyllabic words and get pupils, as a starter, to pronounce the words and discuss what they mean. It could also make a great bit of prediction. When they read the text, they will know the pronunciation and some of the meanings of the words.

Cyclists

These are the long sentences where you often forget what the start of the sentence was about by the time you get to the end.

- Remind pupils that they have to take more care with longer sentences. They might have to go a bit slower with these sentences.

- Sentences that have some of these – ; : , ( ) – might need to be reread.

- Teach pupils how to read these long sentences.

Tractors

These are words that they might not be familiar with. Rather than give the word and its pronunciation, like the fanfare usually given to the unveiling of a plaque, show them the word and get them to pronounce it. Then correct them if necessary. If we don't give them opportunities in simple lessons to explore how to say words, how are we going to help them build their confidence at guessing words that they are not familiar with?

- Give them a short glossary of five to eight words.

- Simplify for the audience.

Passengers

I think we don't do enough one-to-one reading in secondary schools. We seem to think reading something aloud in class is the equivalent. I think it isn't. Personally, I think it can cause more problems than it fixes. It can destroy confidence. Simply, reading to a teacher is so much more effective as it is less public and there isn't so much of an issue if you correct the pupil.

Whilst pupils are on task, get one pupil to do it verbally with you. They could read the text and you question them afterwards. The comments they give you can be written in their exercise book as bullet points. This can be done for the full spectrum of ability and not just those that are weak at reading.[12]

Directed Activities Related to Texts

The word-rich are able to use what they know about language and the world to interact with what they are reading. This helps them to create meaning from the words on the page. Back in the late 1990s, Directed Activities Related to Texts (DARTs) were all the rage and were used widely in many classrooms to help improve word-poor pupils' reading comprehension. Now, not so much. The technique was developed to use reading as a way of learning a 'subject'. Its aim was to foster independent reading and actively engage pupils with texts.

Essentially, DARTs are reading activities designed to help pupils zoom in on, and encourage interaction with, texts and can be based on any kind of reading material. English teachers have traditionally used them to analyse literature but they work equally well with extracts from magazines, newspapers, pamphlets and textbooks; in fact, using DARTs is an easy way to make such texts more interesting and it helps break away from the view that reading is a solitary activity. Instead, DARTs can be used in small groups or pairs.

Now, normally I'm against spending time creating resources because often the time spent has proportionately little impact on learning, but DARTs are often worth it as they really concentrate pupils on thinking about what they're reading. Also, it's worth noting that there's no need for fancy equipment and resources, which might fail horribly in the middle of your carefully crafted lesson.

---

12 Adapted from Chris Curtis's blog post: Deep Reading: Literacy Across the Curriculum, *Learning from My Mistakes* (9 March 2013). Available at: <http://learningfrommymistakesenglish.blogspot.co.uk/2013/03/deep-reading-literacy-across-curriculum.html>.

DARTs can be broadly divided into two groups: reconstruction activities and analysis activities.

Reconstruction activities

Reconstruction activities require pupils to reconstruct a text or diagram by filling in missing words, phrases or sentences, or by sequencing text that has been jumbled. These types of texts take a little bit of time to produce, which is perhaps the main reason they're not used that often. You have to modify the original text by blanking out words, phrases or sentences, or, if you feel you've got loads of spare time on your hands, by cutting the text into segments.

Here are some examples:

- Gap fill – these activities require pupils to understand context and vocabulary in order to identify the correct words (or type of words) that belong in the deleted parts of a text. Words could be deleted randomly or according to various criteria (e.g. all adjectives, all words that have a particular letter pattern). The passage is presented to pupils, who insert the correct words in the gaps to construct appropriate meaning from the text.

- Generation – similar to gap fill, generation requires pupils to generate their own ideas and responses to missing sections of text. Interestingly, generation prompts that require free-response answers are a very good way of getting pupils to remember information.[13]

- Sequencing (arranging jumbled segments of text in a logical or chronological sequence) – this can help pupils understand the importance of coherence and cohesion within a piece of text.

- Grouping – pupils group segments of text according to categories.

....

13 See Lindsey E. Richland, Robert A. Bjork, Jason R. Finley and Marcia C. Linn, Linking Cognitive Science to Education: Generation and Interleaving Effects. In B. G. Bara, L. Barsalou and M. Bucciarelli (eds), *Proceedings of the Twenty-Seventh Annual Conference of the Cognitive Science Society* (Mahwah, NJ: Lawrence Erlbaum, 2005), pp. 1850–1855.

- Table completion – pupils fill in the cells of a table that has row and column headings, or they provide row and column headings where cells have already been filled in.

- Diagram completion – pupils complete an unfinished diagram or label a finished diagram.

- Prediction activities – these help pupils to get an idea of the general organisation, major topics and subtopics of a text. It can involve pupils using the beginning or the appearance (title, headings, illustrations, layout, etc.) of a piece of text to predict what comes next. Following prediction, before reading on, pupils ask themselves questions (e.g. What would I need or want to know about this topic?).

Analysis activities

Analysis activities require pupils to find and categorise information by marking or labelling a text or diagram, and, as they don't require any preparation on your part beyond finding the texts, they're much more straightforward to plan.

Here are some examples:

- Text marking – pupils find and underline parts of the text that have a particular meaning or contain certain information.

- Text segmenting and labelling – pupils break the text into meaningful chunks and label each chunk.

- Table construction – pupils draw a table and use the information in the text to decide on row and column headings and fill in the cells.

- Diagram construction – pupils construct a diagram that explains the meaning of the text (e.g. a flow chart for a text that explains a process, a branch diagram for a text that describes how something is classified).

- Answering comprehension questions – there are different ways to use questioning, such as:

  * The teacher frames the questions.

  * Pupils question each other in pairs or small groups.

  * The teacher asks a thought-provoking high order or open question and asks pupils to consider and discuss.

- Identifying topic sentences – this is usually the first sentence of the paragraph. Focusing on the first sentence of a paragraph gives the reader an idea of what the paragraph is going to be about and can enable them to map complex texts.

- Encouraging pupils to give appropriate headings for each paragraph or section of the text to support them in understanding the whole passage.

- Paraphrasing – pupils put a passage from source material into their own words. This is a particularly useful skill to develop when wanting to borrow from a source without plagiarising.

- Summarising – this involves pupils putting only the main ideas from the source material into their own words, which is an essential skill when making notes.

So, if you're convinced that DARTs are worth a punt, here's a method you can use for creating your own. Firstly, read through your chosen text carefully. As you read, interact with the text. For example, underline or circle important information, write questions raised by the text or that it doesn't answer, list the main ideas and the supporting detail, or draw a table or a diagram.

Then consider whether the text lends itself to a particular type of interaction and develop an appropriate graphic organiser (see pages 156–161). The following table is a useful guide on how to proceed.

Creating graphic organisers for DARTs

Purpose of text	Suggested graphic organiser
Compares and contrasts two or more things	Table or comparison alley
Describes a process	Flow chart
Describes a fictional or non-fictional sequence of events	Flow chart
Classifies an object or concept	Branch diagram
Describes an object	Labelled diagram
Presents an argument	Spider diagram or concept map

Finally, decide whether you want your pupils to do a reconstruction activity or an analysis activity. For example, if you developed a flow chart whilst reading the text and you want pupils to have a go at a reconstruction activity, develop a relevant flow chart and then delete some of the information from the chart. Your pupils will then complete the missing information as they read. Or, if you'd prefer them to have a crack at an analysis activity, simply write instructions to help them construct their own flow chart. There might be several steps in this activity, so you might ask pupils to underline the steps in the process that is being described in the text they are analysing and then create their own flow chart. Either way, the process is fairly foolproof and, as you experiment, you'll get quicker at knocking up fabulous DARTs which you can save and reuse as appropriate.

DARTs have several advantages over 'just reading' a text. When pupils are forced to interact with texts and think about the words and their meanings, their reading comprehension improves. They also become more aware of how texts are structured which, in turn, makes them more critical of what they read. They begin to ask questions about the information that has been included and excluded from the text and about the words and sentence constructions that the writer has chosen. And, as pupils' understanding of how text is constructed improves, so too does their own writing. Crucially, interacting with texts in this way can also teach pupils to avoid plagiarism.

Interaction is a great way to teach academic language to word-poor pupils and can help prepare them for the types of text they'll encounter in different subjects. Normally pupils gloss over nominalised terms and specialist vocabulary but DARTs force them to consider the impact of words and structure in a really empowering way. So, why not give 'em a go?

Independent research

> Our ability to capture the information often exceeds our ability to know what to do with it.
>
> Francis Collins

Independent research, or FOFO,[14] as it's affectionately known, is the fine old tradition of sending children off to copy stuff from the Internet and paste it into a document for them to pass off as their own work. When I were a lad, the World Wide Web was still a distant twinkle in Tim Berners-Lee's eye so we had to look in books. Or ask our mums. However, every teacher knows full well that if we set pupils a project on volcanoes, they'll head straight for Google.

We can teach them about digital literacy, the reliability of sources and various other bits of techno know-how, but unless we're happy with the cut-and-pasted crap that's commonly served up as homework, we need to teach them the ins and outs of proper independent research.

....

14 If you don't know what this means you're welcome to continue reading the footnote but if you're a sensitive flower you may prefer not to. If you're sure, here goes: Fuck Off and Find Out.

So, what does independent research actually mean? Well, first off, it's emphatically not plagiarism. Many pupils, even sixth formers who should know better, really aren't clear on this point!

Good independent research should do two things: firstly, it should show evidence of independent research from varied sources and, secondly, it should result in an original product where you apply what you've learned. This is surprisingly easy to teach; here are the guidelines I use with my pupils, whether they're in Year 7 or Year 13:

1.   Look for information from *at least* three sources.

2.   Cite the sources in full – this means also writing down the URLs.

3.   Summarise what each source says.

4.   Explain what you think based on the information you have uncovered.

5.   Proudly hand in your research on time.

It's also worth spending some time on how to take notes effectively. Here's what I think is important:

- Paraphrase information – record page references and sources.

- Highlight quotations – make sure they're accurate and you know where to find them. Where possible write down page numbers.

- Accuracy matters – not just the accuracy of the quotations; insist that notes are spelt and punctuated correctly. Remember, what we practise we get good at.

I can't stress enough how important it is to do these things at the time you're looking at the information. Incidentally, if I had managed to follow my own advice I would have saved myself many hours in the writing of this book!

I would also recommend teaching pupils how to write a thesis statement. This is essential for many A level courses, but pupils of all ages will benefit from the practice.

A sound thesis is:

- A single arguable point.

- A statement rather than a question.

- Restricted to ideas which you will discuss.

So, if you are given a research topic like this:

> Based on the study of the 2004 Indian Ocean disaster, how might the impact of a tsunami be beneficial to people and their environment?

You could turn it into a thesis statement like this:

> Life in Indonesia is better for women and children because of the 2004 tsunami.

This has several distinct advantages. You'll be much clearer on exactly what it is you are going to research and it will produce a more precise and interesting piece of work.

These simple ideas will improve immeasurably the quality of research your pupils produce, no matter their age or stage. No longer will they simply churn out whatever Wikipedia comes up with. Instead they'll be forced to read carefully, make careful selections and synthesise the information they uncover. What more could we want?

Building a reading culture

Building a reading culture is, I think, the most intractable literacy-related problem. How do you convince unwilling kids to read?

Maya Angelou says, 'Any book that helps a child to form a habit of reading, to make reading one of his deep and continuing needs, is good for him,' and I'm certain this is true. Whilst only texts that enrich pupils' cultural capital should be studied in school, they should be encouraged to read everything and anything in their own time.

Ofsted say that schools should 'develop policies to promote reading for enjoyment throughout the school'.[15] They also complain that too many schools have no coherent policy on reading. Whilst schools are pretty good at putting in place support programmes for weak readers, they're not so good at articulating what makes a good reader. Consequently, many schools have abandoned the promotion of wider reading and reading for pleasure due to the constraints and pressures of covering the curriculum.

Happily, Ofsted also offer all sorts of advice on how to go about developing reading cultures in schools:

> In every school in the survey there were successful measures to involve the library and ensure that the librarian had an important role in developing reading. This is common sense, building on the specialist knowledge that librarians possess. Where librarians are fully integrated into the management structure of the school, they have an opportunity to influence debate and to enhance the library's contribution to pupils' progress. Many of the imaginative programmes to encourage reading that inspectors see are inspired by a good librarian.[16]

> The primary and secondary schools visited emphasised the school library as contributing markedly to improving literacy skills. All the schools visited had well-resourced libraries, often with computerised loan systems and facilities for accessing learning resources on an intranet. Libraries in the secondary schools were often open for much longer than the school day. This enabled students to complete their homework on the school's computers before and after school. The enthusiasm and responsiveness of the librarian generally had a direct impact on the attitudes of the students towards the library and reading.[17]

> The librarian works closely with students through initiatives such as the popular reading group scheme. However, the promotion of reading extends far beyond the school library. The school promotes a wide range of cross-curricular reading events involving different departments. Links with the performing arts and history are especially strong and drama teachers, for example, ensure that students read texts in their lessons. A joint parent/child reading group was launched, attended by a local author who spoke of the importance of parents encouraging their children to

15 Ofsted, *Moving English Forward*, p. 7.

16 Ofsted, *Improving Literacy in Secondary Schools: A Shared Responsibility*. Ref: 120363. Available at: <http://www.ofsted.gov.uk/resources/improving-literacy-secondary-schools-shared-responsibility>, p. 40.

17 Ofsted, *Removing Barriers to Literacy*. Ref: 090237. Available at: <http://www.ofsted.gov.uk/resources/removing-barriers-literacy>, p. 42.

read. Family Review days are held in the library, giving parents the opportunity to talk about books with the librarian and students. Lists of recommended reads are sent home and the school has also produced a leaflet on reading for parents, with tips and hints on supporting your child's reading.[18]

In addition, the Department for Education has asked teachers and librarians for practical, innovative ideas to promote reading in school. This is the list of suggestions they have produced:

- Engage parents by inviting them to become members of the school library, or by inviting them to workshops on how to support their child's reading.

- Make reading visible around the school by displaying attractive posters – 'Good reads for historians …', 'Want to know more about the causes of earthquakes? Try these books …'

- Have sections of a text placed in different corridors and areas so that pupils need to read one and find the next extract.

- Let pupils take home six books from the library over the summer holiday (one for each week). Better that the books are with the pupils than sitting on the shelves over the summer holiday!

- Recruit influential pupils to be book, author or genre 'ambassadors' – with an element of competition to see who can secure the widest readership.

- Try 'Taking a chance on a book' promotions where some books are wrapped in paper to hide their identity; this gives an air of mystery and can encourage readers to try different genres.

- Add small 'recommendation' cards to book displays with lively pupil or teacher comments, or try 'If you like this then you'll love …'

- Encourage other staff to use and promote the library to pupils. One school uses regular 'literary lunches' hosted by the librarian, where new acquisitions are shared with other members of staff.

....

18 Ofsted, *Moving English Forward*, p. 56.

- Take the library out of the library – set up book displays and reading corners in different parts of the school.

- Show pupils how current literature has its roots in the past, e.g. *Twilight* and *Dracula*.

- Take advantage of technology in the school – share book recommendations, extracts or reviews on the school's intranet, screensavers and TV display screens.

- Set up book groups for pupils – encourage them to discuss books and make recommendations, or try shadowing book awards such as the Carnegie.

- Develop a subject-specific 'extension library' to enable older pupils who may be specialising in history or economics to develop their reading repertoire whilst connecting to and making sense of their specialist areas of interest.[19]

Former Children's Laureate, poet and education tinkerer, Michael Rosen, has also suggested a 20-point plan:

1. Improve home–school liaison

2. Hold events

3. Create close links with booksellers

4. Appoint a school librarian

5. Set up school book clubs

6. Share information on local libraries

7. Adopt an author or illustrator

8. Try book-making

9. Share books

10. Read widely

---

19 Department for Education, Encouraging Reading for Pleasure (25 June 2012). Available at: <http://www.education.gov.uk/schools/teachingandlearning/pedagogy/b00192950/encouraging-reading-for-pleasure/practical-ideas-to-promote-reading>, p. 3.

11. Try regular themed activities

12. Get the reading habit

13. Collect odd, old books

14. Keep and use book reviews

15. Avoid hidden catches

16. Have plenty of books around

17. Encourage varied reading

18. Perform stories

19. Share precious books

20. Train colleagues on children's literature[20]

These ideas sound great and are all, I'm sure, worth pursuing. The trick is for schools to get leaders on board and enthusiastic. The Department for Education suggests senior leaders (especially the head teacher) could promote reading by:

- Making it a whole-school priority.

- Ensuring that all teachers promote reading in their subject areas, e.g. historical novels in history.

- Raising the profile of the library/librarian.

- Reading themselves – being a role model – keeping and publishing a reading blog.

- Creating a reading-friendly environment.[21]

20 Each of these tips is fully explained on the Reading Revolution website: <http://www.readingrevolution.co.uk/get-started.html>.

21 Department for Education, Encouraging Reading for Pleasure, p. 4.

If this happens then everything else will follow. But as an individual teacher battling against the tide, it can be very tough. The impact you can have will be more limited but you can still affect the pupils in your classes by:

- Being a role model and reading yourself.

- Interesting pupils in reading by making recommendations, leaving books on desks, talking about books and displaying books in your classroom.

- Engaging with pupils as readers and getting to know their preferences.

- Referring to whole books/literary fiction rather than just chunks in textbooks.

- Displaying posters – 'If you like science, you'll love …' with a list of recommended literary fiction, or 'Mr Didau is currently reading … by …'

Reading fast and slow

Head of English and education writer Alex Quigley discusses how we might go about improving the teaching of reading by 'reading fast and slow':

Few things in my professional life give me more pleasure than the experience of reading to, and with, a class. When I think about my time at school, I can start to piece together fragments of those rapt moments of whole-class reading which no doubt kindled a love for school that resulted in me becoming a teacher. When I now teach the 'class reader' I enjoy it immensely and I love it when pupils groan when we have to stop reading and they have to do some 'real work'! I do, however, have a sense of conflict with the nature of reading and studying the class reader. I think about how we naturally read at pace and at our own volition; how the process is slowed down by 'study'. Then I wonder about the paucity of many of our pupils' experience of reading beyond the annual class reader (boys, in particular, are in danger of falling significantly behind in terms of reading for pleasure and reading attainment), and whether we are killing a potential spark for reading. I then come to thinking about how we can balance the slow study of reading with the pleasure of natural 'fast reading'.

I teach in a school that tries hard to foster a reading culture. The library does some great business with a good proportion of our pupils: pupils read regularly in form time; last year we undertook our own 'Big Read' fundraising, during which we raised thousands of pounds. Our strategies are not an Ofsted tick-box, but a value system, supported wholeheartedly by our school leaders who understand the real value of reading. We clearly value reading. We want our pupils to be 'word-rich' – with all the attendant benefits that brings. Still, it never feels like we are doing enough; at times it feels like a truly Sisyphean task. In our department we ensure that at least one novel is read a year at Key Stage 3, with much poetry and shorter reading besides. We are aiming to slim down our content, deepening and slowing down the assessment process to enhance the learning – and we are looking to cram as much reading into the curriculum as possible. We know the importance of reading for pleasure and being word-rich. What becomes crucially important is how we can boost 'real reading' for many of our pupils who only read that one class reader a year.

For the legion of kids who don't read habitually, the reading we facilitate is paramount. Yet, reading a novel over the course of six weeks, and studying it within an inch of its life, can drain the pleasure away from reading for many pupils. Don't get me wrong, most English teachers work brilliantly to stave off boredom and to enrich the understanding of their pupils, with strategies that also strengthen their reading skills and their worldly knowledge.

Fundamentally, however, we still face the scenario where many pupils are desperate to read on, but we stifle this natural curiosity to stick to the plan and teach reading skills. What might help is to think of different ways to facilitate reading with pupils that better imitate the natural state of reading a great novel – of reading it fast and not pausing for breath, never mind a four-day break between chapters! Perhaps, if we unburden our curriculum we can find more space to read in a more rapid way – in such a way that encourages the natural pace of reading, a high degree of challenge and more independent and interdependent teaching and learning. We could have 'reading weeks' like at university. In my university experience, I learnt more in reading weeks than any other time.

A while back, I talked casually to a colleague in our faculty about what she was doing with her Year 9 group at that moment. She was working with visually stunning images when I dropped into the lesson and I was curious as to what the pictures were and how they were being used. It turned out that she was teaching *Animal Farm* by George Orwell. This wasn't on the 'official' Year 9 plan so I was intrigued. She had simply taken a two-week slot, having found time from our slimmed down content approach, and decided to challenge them with the great Orwell novella. She actually taught it to two classes of varying ability ranges. There was no grand outcome with attendant assessment measures; simply some initial debate, discussion and reading. Lots of reading. By way of celebrating that reading they had created the amazing display. All in a couple of weeks. Fast reading satisfied the pleasure principle of reading much more than our typical approach. It struck me how simple but effective this approach was and how we didn't have to be burdened by the demands of a content-driven curriculum – that we could read just for the sake of it!

Inspired, I am working with my department to construct a Key Stage 3 curriculum that not only embraces Dedicated Improvement and Reflection Time, but also one that dedicates ample time to reading. It's exciting to think that there's possibly more time than we thought. Many of our pupils don't have a love for reading, yet that passion can be so transformative for success in educational settings, so we need to find time to nurture a liking at the very least; help it grow into a passion. It takes whole-school support (not just financial, but a good book stock doesn't come for free) from leadership, from a great school library and support from parents if this pleasure is to be grown and sustained. If we could read at least a book a term, a classic a year, in addition to the class reader, then maybe we could help turn the tide towards reading for pleasure. I'm conscious that doesn't seem overly ambitious – but we hope it would be the tip of the iceberg for more reading for pleasure.

As English teachers we must reflect on our Key Stage 3 curriculum. We must reflect upon our priorities. Yes, there are a multitude of factors outside of our control which inhibit reading for pleasure, but we can only control what we control. The precious curriculum time we possess must be used to engender a pleasure for reading wherever possible. I want to review how we can read more than ever, without waiting for official sanction from Michael Gove. In fact, I could end with his own words which echo my sentiments exactly:

> There is one must-have accessory that no one should be seen without: a book. Books complement any outfit and suit any season. But far too few of us make sure we're carrying one. And we certainly don't follow the first rule of fashion – to work the racks. We're not picking up enough new books, not getting through the classics, not widening our horizons. In short, we're just not reading enough.[22]

Some questions to ask about reading:

- How do we best balance 'fast' and 'slow' reading?

- What is the best approach for the pedagogy of fast reading?

- How do we space out reading throughout our curriculum to ensure pupils develop their reading skills in an optimal way?

- How do we ensure pupils read at least three extended books a year within curriculum time at Key Stage 3 (hopefully encouraging many, many more)?

- How do we create a broad and engaging book stock to satisfy our ambition?

....

22 Michael Gove, We Must Teach Our Children to Love Books Again, *The Telegraph* (31 March 2011). Available at: <http://www.telegraph.co.uk/education/8419855/We-must-teach-our-children-to-love-books-again.html>.

- How do we personalise a range of challenging reading material that is in the 'zone of proximal development' for our pupils?

- How do we get parents to support and engage with the process of reading?

- How do we bridge the knowledge gap between their reading at Key Stages 2 and 3?

- How do we maximise our whole-school approach to literacy to complement the drive for more reading?

- How do we get pupils to read more books that complement other curriculum subjects?[23]

If you can answer these questions in a way that satisfies the complexities of your school then you'll be making a significant impact on the lives of your pupils and will be considered a very good egg indeed.

The importance of cultural capital

Let's face it: we need to know to stuff if we're going to have anything resembling a successful life. But what is it we need to know? As an English teacher, I have a fair bit of pretty arcane knowledge that few others outside my profession and subject specialism would see as useful. Doctors know all kinds of stuff, and they save lives. Surely everything they know is vitally important? Well, if it is I've muddled along without knowing the vast majority of it. The same goes for anyone from greengrocers to figure skaters to lion tamers: the knowledge we have is, largely, only important to us.

---

23 Adapted from Alex Quigley's blog post: Reading Fast and Slow, *Hunting English* (17 February 2013). Available at: <http://www.huntingenglish.com/2013/02/17/reading-fast-and-slow/>.

But what about cultural capital – the idea that some knowledge is important for everyone to know? Pierre Bourdieu extended the idea of capital to encompass knowledge of culture.[24] He argued that whilst we all occupy a position within society, we are not defined only by membership of a social class. More important is the 'capital' we can amass through social relations. Needless to say, this can, and often does, result in inequality.

The more you know, the easier it is to learn. It's no good dismissing knowledge and saying that you can just look it up, because whilst that is undoubtedly true, you need to know a stack of stuff to make sense of whatever it is you've looked up. How much quicker and easier to just know that Copenhagen is the capital of Denmark, or that Vespasian was the Roman Emperor that eventually succeeded the Julio-Claudians and that the Julio-Claudians were a loosely knit family of inbreds, perverts and sociopaths who oversaw the transformation of Rome from a bloated oligarchy to a slightly more streamlined monarchy? Or something like that. Anyway, the point is that I want the curriculum to enrich pupils' cultural capital; to give them access to a broad base of interesting and useful cultural concepts into which they will be able to contextualise new ideas and knowledge in a rich tapestry of learning. To this end, I want to try delivering English through a range of good quality texts that will increase pupils' ability to make links and connections between their cultural heritage and the world in which they live.

Also, what you know informs your ability to think. If you don't know something, you can't think about it. Texts which demand background knowledge which most pupils don't already have will mean valuable time can be spent placing the texts in context and exploring elements of society, history and the literature that the author assumes his audience will have read. Now, I know the pronoun in that last clause will have set some readers' teeth on edge but just because most of our great literature has been written by dead white men is no reason not to study it. Arguably, the more alien the culture of great literature is to your pupils, the more you owe it to them to permit them entry into this foreign country. Simply deciding that 'kids like these' won't understand or be interested is an inexcusable cop-out.

------

24 See Pierre Bourdieu, The Forms of Capital. In John G. Richardson (ed.), *Handbook of Theory and Research for the Sociology of Education* (New York: Greenwood, 1986), pp. 241–258.

This does not necessarily mean that we should only teach the 'canon' (although I do think we need to do some of this), but it does mean that it's not OK to use store-cupboard favourites like Robert Swindells's *Stone Cold* as class readers. Whilst this may be a perfectly enjoyable read, it's not particularly worthy of study. I think even its author would be reasonably content to agree this point. So, whilst we should encourage pupils to read anything and everything, we should only actually *study* texts which build cultural capital.

What I know becomes particularly important when I read. My extensive vocabulary and general knowledge enable me to comprehend texts which might baffle those who know less about the world. Reading is the best way to learn new things. But those who are, perhaps, most in need of knowledge are the least able to obtain it. Joseph Heller wrote a book about this.[25]

My point is that cultural capital is important. It enables us to access society in a way which would be impossible if we didn't know any of this trivia. But it's only important because other people know it and it's useful to show that we share values. And that being the case, it really is some kind of elitist scam designed to protect access to institutions.

Is this a bad thing? Maybe. It is, however, the world we live in. Short of rioting, the only way to affect change is from within. The problem with the stakeholder society is that those without cultural capital don't get to place a stake. So, ante up, learn to speak the language of the ruling elite and tear down the walls from the inside.

---

25 *Catch 22* isn't really about knowledge. Sorry – deliberate cultural reference to illustrate my point.

Some thoughts on silent reading

Silent reading is often the core of a school's reading policy. Apparently it hasn't been around as long as you might think. The fourth century Church leader St Ambrose's reading habits were considered unusual enough for St Augustine to comment:

> When [Ambrose] read, his eyes scanned the page and his heart sought out the meaning, but his voice was silent and his tongue was still. Anyone could approach him freely and guests were not commonly announced, so that often, when we came to visit him, we found him reading like this in silence, for he never read aloud.[26]

Why is this important? Well, ever since I learned to internalise my reading I've been devouring books and developing my interior world. This is a private and mysterious place in which all sorts of surprising things happen. I consider myself to be highly articulate and able to vocalise my thoughts in a way that less articulate folk cannot. My vocabulary allows me to conceptualise abstract thoughts because I'm not groping for the words needed to express myself; they're there, waiting. But the swirl of thought beneath this is numinous and liminal (I'm just showing off now). This process is going on (I think) inside everyone, but only those with sufficient words can dip into it and pull out something useful which can be expressed and shared. The point is that I value silent reading very much. I am, however, not a fan of silent reading *in the classroom*.

Doing a spot of research led me to this list of reasons why silent reading should be undertaken in the classroom.

- To help you read faster.

- To improve understanding.

- To help you ignore words you don't need.

- To allow you to reread.

- To help you read whole words at once.

---

26 St Augustine, *Confessions*, Book 6, chapter 3.

- To move quickly to the information you need.

- To involve all the students.

- To give a good model.

- To help with exam practice.

- To help your confidence.

- To help your listening comprehension.

- To give realistic pronunciation practice.

- To concentrate pronunciation on one thing at a time.[27]

I have no real issue with any of these points – they're all worthy aims. My concern is that silence may not be conducive to understanding. As a highly literate individual, I'm capable of deft and subtle understanding of a text and I am able to absorb information rapidly. The word-poor don't share this advantage.

As we've seen, pupils who are good readers experience more success, which makes them want to read more. As they read more, they become even more successful at reading. Their vocabulary and comprehension grows. Hey presto! A virtuous circle. Readers who struggle with decoding or who have poor vocabularies are unlikely to want to expose these weaknesses by picking up a book. They get much less practice and the gap opens up and widens. Silent reading is a lovely experience for the word-rich – they can pick up their current read and crack on. For the word-poor it becomes an exercise in trying to disguise the fact that they're holding the book upside down. The role of the teacher becomes that of Reading Police, penalising poor readers for non-compliance.

Maybe I've been damaged by my experience of reading lessons coupled with Accelerated Reader. This is a computer program that tests pupils' reading ability and categorises books into levels of difficulty. Children are expected to read books within their 'reading range' and then take a multiple-choice quiz to prove they've

---

27 From ELT Teacher's Corner: Silent Reading in Class (11 June 2012). Available at: <http://www.teachers-corner.co.uk/silent-reading-in-class/>.

read the damn thing. They then get points equal to the value of the perceived difficulty of the book. And you know what points mean? Now if 'all you want is to look into a classroom and see a class full of wee kids reading then Accelerated Reader is your man'.[28] But, if you're interested in developing lifelong readers, it ain't gonna work any more than any other system of extrinsic rewards will affect behaviour beyond the immediate to short term.

The best way of getting all pupils to read involves them having conversations about reading and books. 'Reading journals' in which pupils engage in a conversation with their teacher about what they read could be one way of making this work. There's a very real benefit in this kind of interaction, but the bit that makes it work isn't the silence. It's the conversation. Some schools start English lessons with 10 minutes of silent reading. And whilst there's no way I'd want to dismiss teachers' positive experiences of this kind of activity, I think the key element in what makes this successful isn't necessarily the silence. Rather, it's about teachers' commitment to and value of personal reading. Of course, we must be involved in pupils' reading, but should this involvement happen in silence?

We all agree that getting kids reading is a good thing and there are loads of well-meaning approaches designed to make this happen – Sustained Silent Reading (SSR) and Drop Everything And Read (DEAR) to name but two. The problem with these programmes is that if we want pupils to read lots then we need to teach them to read well. This means we have to make implicit reading skills explicit. Silent reading *looks* like a good idea because it gives pupils the time and space needed to read. What it doesn't do is help poor readers become more fluent, and is therefore doomed to failure.

I believe communication is the key to the successful teaching of reading. Hirsch suggests that, 'In the classroom, the teacher can and should ask children frequently to make formal prepared and unprepared presentations to the class.'[29] So, high quality speaking and listening that develop pupils' control of language and broaden their vocabulary is fundamental to reading.

28 Kenny Pieper's blog post: Time, Choice and Love – What Makes a Reader?, *Just Trying To Be Better Than Yesterday* (22 May 2013). Available at: <http://justtryingtobebetter.net/time-choice-and-love-what-makes-a-reader/>.

29 Hirsch, *The Knowledge Deficit*, p. 31.

I like the idea of reading lessons in which excitement about books is the focus. We want children to enjoy reading, not to suffer it in silence, so let's celebrate it. Let's make it exciting and interactive. Let's read aloud and then stop at a cliffhanger. Let's put on literary festivals. Let's call it something silly like Loud Reading or Noisy Reading. Let's be imaginative and have a go at strategies that might not work, but which stand a better chance than doing something that definitely won't work for the silent legions of the word-poor.

Chapter 6
Writing

If you want to be a writer, you must do two things above all others: read a lot and write a lot. There's no way around these two things that I'm aware of, no shortcut.

Stephen King

Writing basics

Much of the writing produced by pupils in school is rubbish. As long as it demonstrates that they've understood the content they've been taught we are, generally, perfectly happy. But this will embed terrible habits. If we were to shift the focus away from *what* they're writing on to *how* they're writing, we would be able to demonstrate not only that we are explicitly teaching writing skills, but our pupils would start to show a better understanding of the content they're grappling to get to grips with.

Here are three simple techniques to make explicit the process of writing in any lesson where pupils are expected to write.

1. Varying sentences

One of the simplest ways to improve pupils' writing is to ask them to vary their sentences. English teachers often try to complicate this by referring to simple, compound and complex sentences. It's worth knowing what these terms mean but if they are getting in the way of teachers showing pupils how to write more effectively then the terminology can be avoided. Here are some simple suggestions on how to vary sentences:

- **Use long and short sentences.** The length of your sentences has a strong effect on the style of your piece of written work. Short sentences offer impact and clarity whereas long sentences are good when the reader has time to think about the piece of work. But beware of the comma splice – if sentences run on for too long they become increasingly difficult to follow. A simple rule here is to take out all your commas and replace them with full stops. If this isn't possible then the comma is probably necessary.

- **Avoid overusing 'and' or 'but'.** Pupils can be tempted to write ever expanding sentences by adding clause after clause connected with these simple conjunctions. If we tell them not to do this then they won't. The one time it is worth using these words is at the beginning of sentences. Children are taught not to do this in primary school, for some reason, but they can be used to make writing more cohesive and to add impact.

- **Vary sentence starts.** All too often pupils default to beginning sentences with 'I' or 'The'. This is fine occasionally but quickly becomes dull. It is much better to explicitly teach pupils to begin sentences with words ending with '-ly', '-ed' and '-ing'.

Tired old sentences will be pepped up by using some of these simple techniques and pupils' writing will be transformed into something you might actually want to read.

2. Using discourse markers

An even simpler way to improve writing is to employ a range of discourse markers. These handy phrases give writing shape and direction; crucially they make it easier for readers to understand your thought processes. And, most importantly, they make you sound clever.

Share the following list with pupils in advance of writing and get them to select the discourse markers they could use to connect their thoughts:

Adding	and, also, as well as, moreover, too
Cause and effect	because, so, therefore, thus, consequently
Sequencing	next, then, first, finally, meanwhile, before, after
Qualifying	however, although, unless, except, if, as long as, apart from, yet
Emphasising	above all, in particular, especially, significantly, indeed, notably
Illustrating	for example, such as, for instance, as revealed by, in the case of
Comparing	equally, in the same way, similarly, likewise, as with, like
Contrasting	whereas, instead of, alternatively, otherwise, unlike, on the other hand

Know your discourse markers

3. Demystifying spelling

Here's a confession: I'm not very good at spelling. Interestingly, it's as socially acceptable to admit to being a poor speller as it is to own up to being bad at maths. It almost seems to carry a certain cachet. At age 14, I was taken in hand by Mr Birch, my English teacher, who was determined that I would learn to spell.

He told me that he would refuse to accept my excuses and that his expectation was 100% accuracy!

And now I can spell. It's my contention that most people who are considered good spellers simply know some of the same tricks and tips that I am about to share. The advice Mr Birch gave to me was that I should design a strategy for every word that I commonly misspelt. He advocated thinking about what words look like and sound like and using mnemonics.

There are various alternatives to this approach, the most common being the dreaded spelling test. Both my daughters come home once a week with a list of spellings to learn. The older daughter cares deeply about pleasing her teacher and works hard to learn her spellings, and every week she gets them all right. Whenever I go through her school books, though, her work is littered with misspellings of these very same words. Somehow, despite having learned how to spell these words for a test, she still doesn't know how to spell them when it comes to writing in context. My younger daughter is the exact opposite: she can't be bothered to learn spellings and, consequently, she rarely gets more than half of them right. Strangely, though, she seems to make fewer spelling mistakes than her sister when it comes to her written work.

Now, I accept that trying to generalise from such a small sample is fraught with all kinds of difficulties, but it strikes me that learning spellings out of context seems not to work. Instead, I'd suggest compiling a list of words which are frequently misspelled and teaching pupils spelling strategies based on mnemonics and what these words look and sound like.

What words look like

Everyone knows that there's a rat in 'sep **a rat** e', but I find it quietly profound that there is a lie in what we 'be **lie** ve'.

What words sound like

Up until I was 14 years old, I spent one twelfth of every year writing 'Febuary' into my exercise books. Before Mr Birch, I can't remember any other teacher pointing out this common mistake. He explained that the word was 'Feb-**ru**-ary', and that if I sounded it out as I wrote it I would never forget it. And I haven't. Now for one twelfth of every year I say Feb-ru-ary to myself as I write the date on the board. There are lots of words which benefit from this approach: govern-ment, envi-ron-ment, Wed-nes-day and so on.

Mnemonics

My favourite way of learning spellings is to create mnemonics. There are some great ones for tricky words like 'necessary' (**N**ever **E**at **C**hips, **E**at **S**alad **S**and-wiches **A**nd **R**emain **Y**oung) but one of my favourites is the mnemonic I've learned for spelling 'rhythm'. I always used to have to check this before writing it on the board. A few years ago a little lad in Year 8 jumped up and said, 'It's easy, sir: rhythm helps your two hips move!' I've never had to check it from that day to this.

And for English teachers here is a real gift:

Close your eyes and imagine **P**inky **O**range **E**lephants **I**n **A**frica.

You will never ever have to look up how to spell onomatopoeia again!

Whenever you find spelling mistakes in pupils' work, get them to come up with a trick to help them learn how to spell the word correctly; their creativity will amaze you.

How to get pupils to value writing

How are most children taught writing? Badly.

Pupils do a lot of writing at school but, bless me, most of it is turgid, error strewn and unloved. In practically every lesson they're required to scribble stuff in their exercise books, even if it's only a learning objective and the date. Having spent a good deal of time observing lessons across the curriculum, I can safely say that most of the writing pupils do is an exercise in missed opportunities. And almost none of this writing is valued in any way other than that it indicates whether or not they've understood what you were teaching.

Why is this? Why do we get kids to 'write down what you've learned today' without the slightest interest in how they're supposed to write it, whether it will be spelt or punctuated correctly, or even if it will be organised into sentences? I'll tell you why: because it's easy. If pupils are writing, they're busy. If they're busy, they're not fiddling with Bunsen burners or twanging rulers. And there's the added bonus that you can then have a peek in their books to see whether, in fact, they did learn anything. And that's fair enough, as far as it goes. It's not that I'm advocating that pupils do less writing, rather that their writing should be valued – by us as much as them.

I want to see the end of purposeless writing that exists solely to convey content knowledge. My feeling is that whenever we ask pupils to transcribe their thoughts without considering how we want them to do it, we're actively doing them a disservice. We're participating in a conspiracy that says: 'It doesn't matter how you write. No, spelling's not that important! Apostrophes? Pah! Who cares?'

What pupils are learning, day in, day out, is that writing, well, just doesn't matter.

Success criteria for writing

Even when writing does purport to have a purpose, it's often bizarre. One of the saddest examples I've seen in a pupil's book was this: 'Write a letter to a scientist explaining what you know about osmosis.' Why? Who would ever write like this? Is that really the best we can come up with? And what was worse was that there had evidently not been even the vaguest attempt to explore the conventions of letter writing.

One of the most effective and simplest examples of literacy teaching I've seen this year was in a maths lesson where the teacher asked the pupils to reflect on their learning using sentence stems displayed on the wall and then asked them to proofread what they'd written. This is so easy that any teacher could do it without breaking a sweat.

Moving up a gear, one of my favourite examples of success criteria being used to teach writing explicitly is this:

- Technical language (e.g. invertebrate).

- Probability words used.

- Data is quoted – precise.

- Comparisons made.

- Clarity (e.g. variety, fewer words).

- Sentences should (try to) join ideas.

- Commas to separate different parts of the idea/concept.

This list comes courtesy of science teacher extraordinaire, Darren Mead.[1] It's abundantly clear from this list that he puts a lot of thought into designing success criteria which focus on both how and why pupils are being asked to write

---

1   These are Darren's success criteria from a science lesson. For more insights visit his wonderful blog, Sharing Pedagogical Purposes: <http://pedagogicalpurposes.blogspot.co.uk/>.

like scientists. Why can't every piece of writing pupils are expected to do be as carefully considered?

Well, I'm not entirely unreasonable; sometimes we have good reasons for wanting short bursts of writing to be completed quickly. But when this is the case we should take care to tell pupils so. And when writing is to be taken seriously, tell pupils they are *drafting* rather than writing. The first time anything is written it is a draft. This sends a clear message that it will be redrafted. Possibly more than once. For short, straightforward pieces of content writing I only insist that writing should be proofread.

Proofreading

Now, whilst on the subject of proofreading, I'd like to share some of my thinking about many of the marking notation guides I've seen in circulation. Most of them are fiendishly thorough and cover an endless variety of possible errors. If you're using something like this, please stop. It is, on the whole, pointless. It will only be fully understood by a few grammarians who don't need it anyway and be rightly ignored by everyone else, pupils included. At my previous school, the then literacy coordinator, Dee Murphy, came up with the PCS Code. This simple document covered the basics – punctuation, capital letters and spelling – whilst simultaneously sharing the same initials as the school. It was simple enough to be both memorable and useful. I have shamelessly plundered its wisdom for my current school and rebranded it as the CSP Code. Ingenious, eh?

CSP Code
Clevedon School Proofreading Code
Literacy marking for students and teachers

'If it's not proofread, it's not finished.'
C – Capital letters
S – Spelling
P – Punctuation
// – Paragraphs
? – doesn't make sense

The idea is that pupils are expected to seek out and correct errors before submitting work for marking. If I then spot anything they've missed (woe betide them!), I use the CSP notation to point it out before asking them to redraft.

It takes time and effort to train pupils to do this willingly and thoroughly. They will attempt to wear you down by continuing in their callow disregard for accurate writing. But know this: they will thank you for your finicky perseverance in the end. And if they don't, they'll at least be able to write accurately, so hah!

Writing alongside your pupils

Another way to increase the status of any writing task you set your pupils is to also do it yourself. Whenever I set a piece of extended writing, I write my own. I was first advised to do this about six years ago and I've been a zealous convert ever since. Writing alongside pupils has several advantages. Firstly, they can't ask you questions and are forced to rely on their own resources for the duration of the task. As soon as their little hands start to creep up, I just tell them that I'm busy writing and, for the most part, this seems reasonable to them. Of course, I provide help in the form of clear success criteria and stuck stations around the room, which they can consult if confounded.

It's also a great way to model the thinking required to write in a particular way. The benefits are huge; not only do I now have a vast resource bank of essays I've written, it's also made me more effective at teaching various aspects of the curriculum. Because I've experienced the same difficulties, I know what problems my pupils are likely to encounter. Sometimes I've realised that a particular task is too hard (or too easy) and have been able to adjust my teaching as a result. Sometimes the benefits have been particularly dramatic. When I taught the spoken language component of the English Language GCSE course for first time, it wasn't until I'd got halfway through my controlled assessment that I realised what I should have taught. Would I have realised this without doing the work? Maybe not.

Sometimes I type my work and project it on the wall, either whilst pupils are working or after they've finished. Sometimes I give them typed copies to read and mark. Sometimes I read my work aloud. The point is that they know I can do what I'm asking them to do and do it well. Admittedly, sometimes too well – I've had to learn how to put together 'perfect' C grade essays as well as A*s.

So, to sum up, here are three simple techniques for getting pupils to value their writing:

- Give clear success criteria on the Genre, Audience and Purpose (GAP) of the writing they will be using.

- Focus on the process of drafting and make sure you give lesson time for them to redraft and improve written work.

- Write alongside pupils in order to raise the importance and value of the task.

Thinking like a writer

How do we get better at writing? By writing.

The advice I always give to pupils to improve their writing is to write. Often. Every day if possible. This might be a private diary entry, an Amazon review, an essay or, even better, a public blog post which someone might actually read.

For years now I've been in the habit of writing with my pupils. Whenever they have a controlled assessment to write or a question to answer, I do the work too.

But the biggest (and most unexpected) benefit has been that my own writing has improved enormously. The hours of deliberate practice I've logged in consciously writing A* essays has helped me along the path to mastery. There's a hell of a long way to go before I might consider myself a master but I have started to think of myself as a writer. And that's important. Writing for an audience, drafting and redrafting, and reading critically have been revelatory – when I sit down to write I find that I really am thinking like a writer. But can you teach this?

How, in short, can we best teach pupils to think meta-cognitively about writing?

The more you know about a subject, the better your thinking will be on that subject. Thinking depends on knowledge. I'm sorry if this makes you uneasy, but it just does. That being the case, in order to think like a writer you have to know as much as possible about writing. This knowledge might be broken down into these four components:

1. Awareness of audience and purpose – being clear on why you're writing and who you're writing for.

2. The ability to closely analyse writing (see zooming on pages 100–102).

3. Paragraphing and structure.

4. Spelling, punctuation and grammar.

Pupils need to be exposed to a wide variety of great writing in order to consciously examine how it works. They need the opportunity to explicitly apply this knowledge to texts and then to transfer what they find to their own writing. And they need this experience to be as difficult as possible.

What's that? Isn't it our job to make things easy for pupils? No. It isn't. According to John Hattie: 'A teacher's job is not to make work easy. It is to make it difficult. If you are not challenged, you do not make mistakes. If you do not make mistakes, feedback is useless.'[2]

I'm constantly reminding pupils that certain writing basics can make a big difference to the way their writing is perceived:

● Avoid starting sentences with 'I' or 'The'.

● If in doubt, leave commas out.

● Link paragraphs together with connectives.

And so on …

---

2   Quoted in Warwick Mansell, Pupil–Teacher Interaction, *TES* (1 June 2009). Available at: <http://www.tes.co.uk/article.aspx?storycode=6005411>.

But Robert Bjork talks about the likelihood that long-term retention and transfer of knowledge increases when we remove aids to recall.[3] Clearly this is counter-intuitive, but one of the many things I've learned about cognitive psychology is how unreliable my intuition is. Bjork argues that retrieval-induced forgetting (providing prompts or cues) actively makes it harder to remember anything except the thing that has been prompted. So, if I asked you think of a fruit and told you it began with the letters 'or-' you would immediately think of oranges. But, intriguingly, you would find it much harder to think of apples, bananas or raspberries. Clearly, this is unimportant with something as banal as fruit, but perhaps prompting pupils to pay attention to apostrophes prevents them from also thinking about discourse markers? And, if this is correct, where does that leave us?

Well, we're left where we started: trying to promote domain-specific thinking. One way to make this kind of thinking reflexive is to drill it. The best sports people don't just play their sport, they drill particular aspects in order to improve their performance in one (possibly tiny) area. Daisy Christodoulou, somewhat unfashionably, recommends decontextualised grammar drilling for exactly this reason.[4] If the habits of grammar are ingrained in long-term memory, then working memory is freed up to think about lovelier stuff, like imagery.

As we've seen in our discussion of the teaching sequence for developing independence, another aspect of promoting the kind of thinking engaged in by a writer is to model it. So, how do I think when I write? Here are some of the things I'm aware of consciously thinking about when composing a blog post:

- What is this like to read? Am I being boring? Do I sound too worthy or authoritative? What can I do to make my writing more informal and chatty?

- Is there an extended metaphor I can use to provide a compelling, memorable image?

....

3   Robert A. Bjork, Long-Term Memory [video] (n.d.). Available at: <http://gocognitive.net/interviews/retrieval-induced-forgetting>.

4   Blog post by Daisy Christodoulou, Why and How We Should Teach Grammar, *The Curriculum Centre Blog* (5 February 2012). Available at: <http://www.thecurriculumcentre.org/blog/2012/02/05/why-and-how-we-should-teach-grammar/>.

- Are my sentences sufficiently varied? If so, can I use punctuation to further vary the effect?

- Will exaggeration add humour or make me sound like an idiot?

- Is there a better word than this? Have I already used this phrase? Is there another way of saying this?

- Have I spelt that correctly?

- Is this as good as it could be?

As you can see, this thinking breaks down into my four areas of knowledge about writing (see page 149). This is a process I can (and do) make visible to my pupils but I'm very aware that however much they see me do it, they still need to put in the hard work of doing it themselves.

Two things I enjoy about teaching A level English Language are, first, that pupils have to write a commentary on their own writing. It's a great shame that this isn't something they normally do up until then; making them analyse their writing makes quite a difference to its quality. The second thing is the expectation that they will create multiple drafts. Understanding that writers draft their work is transformative; little of quality is produced at the first attempt. As I well know, achieving mastery in writing cannot be achieved in the short term. It takes effort, determination and time. As legendary American football coach, Vince Lombardi, was quoted in an interview as saying, 'Practice doesn't make perfect. Only perfect practice makes perfect,' but not necessarily better. Just doing the same old thing leads to repeating the same mistakes and bad habits. This, perhaps, is why so many pupils fail to punctuate and use capital letters. Maybe, with a healthy dose of grit and deliberate practice, even the most reluctant can learn to take pleasure in the act of thinking like a writer.

We can encourage pupils to think meta-cognitively about writing in the following ways:

- Teach pupils knowledge about writing.

- Get them reading great texts.

- Model the process of writing and thinking about writing.

- Think counter-intuitively.

- Know when to withdraw scaffolds.

- Never accept the first draft.

Thinking like a subject specialist

But for the most part we don't want our pupils to just think about writing. What we really want is for them to be good scientists, historians, artists and technologists. We want them to understand our subjects and be able to prove this understanding so that we can assess it and say, 'Jolly good, now learn …'

It doesn't take a genius to see that these aims are entirely compatible. As we've already seen, if we can get our pupils to speak using the academic language of our subjects then we will change their thinking. And if their thinking is more akin to a subject specialist's, so too will be their writing. Our pupils will only be able to write like this when their understanding of both content and text types is robust. Shallow knowledge will result in flimsy writing. The key is to work out the structures and nominalisations you want your pupils to be able to use. So, how does a geographer think? What might a mathematician say? And how does a historian write?

Text types

Whilst there are loads of lovely informal ways to write, academic disciplines tend to have distinct demands on how texts should be presented.

Genre pedagogy suggests that there are a number of genres and types of text. In the national curriculum for English, this insight has become bastardised as Writing Triplets. The non-fiction triplets were Persuade, Argue, Advise, and Describe,

Inform, Explain. These were the work of the devil and the less we say about them, the better.

In the very useful *Talk for Writing across the Curriculum*, Pie Corbett and Julia Strong identify six commonly used text types – recount, instruction, information, explanation, persuasion and discussion – and suggest they contain the following features:

Recount

- Select the most interesting events.

- Use detail to help the reader 'see' what happened.

- Add in interesting extra information or comments.

Instruction

- Work out the correct order of instructions so that readers will be able to do whatever it is you are instructing them in – numbered or bulleted points may be helpful.

- Keep the instructions clear and to the point. Diagrams may help the reader.

Information

- Select facts with care so that essential information is included as well as information that will interest the reader.

- Use diagrams and images to illustrate key points.

- Commentary and personal views can make the writing more personal and show enthusiasm.

Explanation

- Diagrams and images can help make the explanation clear and easy to understand.

- Comment on why the explanation might be useful to the reader.

Persuasion

- Decide on the best way to persuade the reader – will they need facts or will you appeal to their feelings?

- Try using counter-arguments to undermine objections the reader might raise.

- Give clear reasons, helpful facts and explain why something might be important.

Discussion

- Try to see events from the point of view of the reader.

- Explain why the topic is important.

- Make sure your argument is fair and balanced.

- Talk to the reader, in order to draw them into thinking about the subject.

The problem with approaching the teaching of texts in this way is that they don't always fit neatly into academic disciplines. In fact, they don't really fit into real texts. Take this book for instance – what text type is it? As far as I can tell it contains elements of all of them, so how helpful is it to teach pupils the elements of discrete text types to use across the curriculum? Much better for all subjects to teach the particular text types they require pupils to be familiar with.

English, depending on whether we're discussing literature or language, can either be a highly specialised academic discipline requiring specialised domain knowledge, or a smorgasbord of interdisciplinary guff. Literature essays are discursive and analytical. They require pupils to be able to zoom in on a writer's technique and zoom out onto the context and meaning of the text being discussed. Essays benefit from being nominalised, from carefully selecting textual references and from being able to synthesise historical, social and literary knowledge with a clear line of opinion on the writer's intentions. Teachers have tried to boil these skills down to oversimplified scaffolds like PEE (Point, Evidence, Explain) or FLIRT (Form, Language, Imagery, Rhythm and Tone) and whilst these may be useful in making pupils familiar with the basic structure of a literature essay, they do little to prepare them for the subtleties of writing analytically about a work of literature. Language essays tend to revert to the requirements of the Writing Triplets and this, sadly, is the one area where pupils may benefit from being drilled in the six text types above.

Mathematicians don't really have to produce texts until long after they've finished school, but they do have to understand them. Maths has its own distinct vocabulary and many pupils fall down on their ability to access so-called 'functional' maths questions, which intersperse pseudo real-world problems with mathematical notations and command words. Clearly, pupils have to be familiar with the text type they will need to access; they could perhaps benefit from creating their own test papers using the conventions they identify from their deconstruction of past papers.

The common genres found in geography, history and science are included in Appendix 4, but other subjects will have their own peculiar requirements. If you're unsure about the text types used in your subject area, an excellent starting place is to look at the texts pupils will need to produce in their exams and other assessments and map them against the text types on pages 153–154.

Graphic organisers

In order to get the best out of our pupils, we should scaffold their writing with graphic organisers. These provide simple visual aids to help organise their ideas. Depending on the type of writing we want pupils to attempt, we should provide different organisers. If we want pupils to compare and contrast different ideas or objects, we can use comparison alley; flow charts are great at providing clear sequences and breaking writing down into manageable chunks; and timelines can capture linear or circular sequences.

Comparison alley[5]

When planning a comparison of two or more items, it's useful to be able to list the similarities and differences of said items in order to make the writing we intend to do as clear and complete as we can. I used to use Venn diagrams to visually represent these comparisons but the problem was always that the overlap between the sets wasn't big enough and everything got a bit squashed in the middle. If we're going to use a graphic organiser we want it to be clear and helpful and so, to that end, I'd recommend using comparison alley instead. For the uninitiated, it looks something like this:

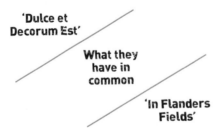

Comparison alley used to compare First World War poems

....

5   Adapted from an idea on the Project for Enhancing Effective Learning website: <http://www. peelweb.org>.

Or this:

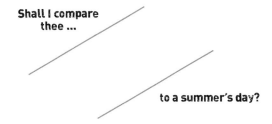

Shall I compare thee ...

to a summer's day?

Comparison alley to compare metaphor

As you can see, unlike Venn diagrams there's acres of room to cram in all the points of similarity your heart could desire.

Timelines

A timeline represents the chronological order of events. It's a handy way to sequence ideas – these could be the order in which they unfolded in an experiment, what happened in the build-up to the Second World War, the chapters of a book or instructions for baking cup cakes. A well-organised timeline helps us to see at a glance how items relate to each other in terms of what followed what.

A fun activity to generate a timeline is that hoary old chestnut, Six Degrees of Separation. If you've never encountered this before, it's based on the idea that every human being in the world is connected to every other human being through no more than six degrees of separation. Maybe so. For our purposes, though, we provide pupils with a prompt connected to the topic we're studying, give them an end point they have to connect to and get them to sequence what they know:

1. Select a topic or theme.

2. Write 1–6 along a timeline.

3. Put your topic at number 6.

4.   Get from the stimulus to your topic in no more or less than six steps.

And we can easily adjust the challenge associated with this by insisting on more or fewer degrees of separation. We could also add in staging posts – for example, 'Your fourth stage must be …'

Flow charts

If we want to break big ideas down into their component parts, a flow chart is the way to go. Flow charts are often used to show multiple possibilities stemming from a single starting point, but in terms of organising writing they're better at representing cause and effect.

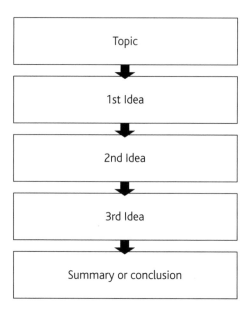

Flow chart

Thinking squares

If you want pupils to be able to connect what they know in new and interesting ways, you could try using my old favourite, thinking squares.[6] The idea is to prompt pupils to see the relationships between items of knowledge in order to make abstract leaps.

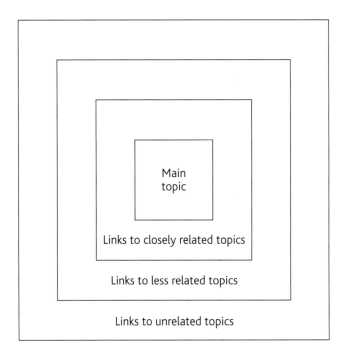

Thinking squares

6   Adapted from question squares in David Didau, *The Perfect (Ofsted) English Lesson* (Carmarthen: Independent Thinking Press, 2012), p. 124.

Hexagons

Another old friend is the trusty hexagon. Using hexagons to connect ideas is a wonderful way to make relationships visible.[7] Why hexagons? Because they've got six sides and when you give a pile of them to kids their natural response is to start fitting them together and making connections. You can put whatever you want on the hexagon or leave them blank for pupils to fill in.

It's almost impossible for pupils not to start making links and this practically guarantees that they will demonstrate a relational understanding of whatever topic they're learning about. The connections made will depend on how much the pupils already know about the topic they're studying. Once they have fitted the hexagons together they have an instant graphic representation of how to structure their writing.

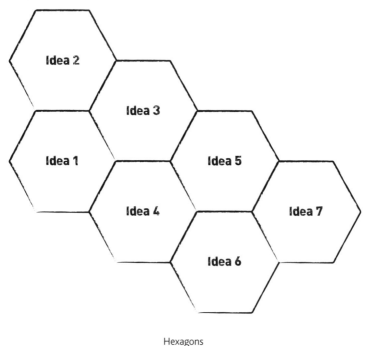

Hexagons

....

7   Also from Didau, *The Perfect (Ofsted) English Lesson*, pp. 96-100.

The beauty of using hexagons is that it forces pupils to decide how they will structure their writing and shows them that there is no single right way to organise their ideas.

Slow Writing

A lot of the writing pupils do in school is rushed. The limitations of timetabling and the inevitability of timed examinations make this almost inevitable. Given an hour to answer a question, most pupils' default position is to race into it, cram in as much verbiage as possible and then down tools to watch the clock tick away the purgatory of the exam hall. This is not a great strategy for producing great writing. So, we teach them to plan and to proofread in the hope that maybe, just maybe, they'll approach their writing more thoughtfully and produce something that won't make their poor teacher groan in anguished suffering.

But is less perhaps more? Over the past few years I've been experimenting with what, for want of a better idea, I'm calling Slow Writing. The idea is to get pupils to slow the hell down and approach each word, sentence and paragraph with love and attention. Obviously they'll write less but what they do write will be beautifully wrought and finely honed.

Here's how it works. Firstly, I tell pupils that I want them to double-space their writing. They find this inordinately difficult so I've taken to providing them with double spaced paper to get them into the habit. I then give them a topic and ask them to complete a set of seemingly random exercises. For example:

1. Your first sentence must start with a present participle (that's a verb ending in '-ing').

2. Your second sentence must contain only three words.

3. Your third sentence must contain a semicolon.

4. Your fourth sentence must be a rhetorical question.

5. Your fifth sentence must start with an adverb.

6. Your sixth sentence must contain a simile.[8]

And so on.

The point of it is that they have to write slowly in order to think about the technique. Generally speaking, pupils find it straightforward to write *what* they want but it's much harder for them to think about *how* they're going to write it. This process forces them to concentrate on the how instead of the what.

Once they've finished, they get to improve it. This is where the double spacing comes into its own. I ask them to interrogate every single word and consider whether there might be a better word. They look at every sentence and ask: could it begin differently? Should it be longer or shorter? Are they absolutely sure it makes sense?

We then examine our paragraphs. The paragraph should be considered the basic unit of writing; it is where the source of coherence begins and the space where words transcend their individual meanings. A well-constructed paragraph helps to map our intentions; it will insist that our thoughts are organised and help prevent us wandering off topic. We must consider how our paragraphs link together: do they flow logically? Does each paragraph pick up where the preceding one leaves off? Is there variety?

Hopefully, they will now be busily scribbling all over their draft and putting the new ideas in the acres of space made available by double spacing their writing. A neat and tidy exam script is one which has not been perfected, is full of mistakes and will get a lower grade.

Other Slow Writing ideas include:

● Popping a load of different sentence instructions into a hat and giving everyone a random selection.

....

8   And if this sounds a tad labour intensive, the highly talented David Riley has produced a piece of free software on his Triptico platform to randomly generate Slow Writing sentence prompts for primary and secondary pupils: <http://www.triptico.co.uk/media/temp/slowWriting.html>. See also Appendix 1 for a suggested list of Slow Writing sentence prompts.

- Giving pupils lists of numbers and telling them that the number of words in their sentences must conform to these numbers.

- Paired writing – get pupils to write alternate sentences and question each other about their choices.

- Use a professionally written text on a different subject and get pupils to copy the structure and techniques.

And the impact? Well, not only do pupils perform better in exams, they're much more confident and experimental and the writing they produce is hugely improved.

As always, the proof of the writing is in the reading. Here's an example of an opening paragraph from a film review of *Twilight* written using Slow Writing:

> Ah, Twilight. That time of day when the boundaries between night and day begin to blur. The moment when the sun begins to set and when all those things that go bump in the night stretch, yawn and start feeling that unbearable urge to pee. The very name is a clue to understanding what this film is all about – you see, it's not one thing or another. It's not just happy daytime romance and it's definitely not all night-time terror. Just like the name implies it's somewhere in between. So, is this a strength or a weakness? You could take the view that it's this quality that helps the film to appeal to as wide an audience as possible: you get the chick-flick crowd as well as the Goths. Or, on the other hand, does it make the whole thing impossibly and disastrously diluted?

Pretty good, huh? I'm sure none of this is particularly original but it's certainly helped me to help my pupils to see writing as something that can, and should, be consciously crafted.

And guess what? Slow Writing techniques could also be used to help pupils craft more sophisticated responses to reading comprehension. Normally, when pupils are asked to respond to questions, their responses are only valued for the content knowledge they convey. But what if we taught them to construct beautifully crafted responses instead?

Here's an example from a design technology test:

> What are the main advantages of using an operational amplifier like the Darlington transistor circuit?

We could scaffold pupils' attempts to craft a response that expresses more complex thoughts by asking them to respond like this:

> Because _____, _____.
> Reasons for using   Main effect(s) of using
> the Darlington transistor circuit   the Darlington transistor circuit

Or what about this geography question:

> Why are the effects of droughts worse in less economically developed countries (LEDCs) than more economically developed countries (MEDCs)?

If we taught pupils to write a sentence beginning with 'Despite', would they produce a more interesting response?

Here's an example from a biology exam:

> Farm animals give off large amounts of methane. Explain the effects of adding large amounts of methane to the atmosphere.

Would the response be more sophisticated if we asked pupils to begin their response with 'Considering that …'?

Clearly, the quality of pupils' answers will still depend on their knowledge and understanding of the subjects they're studying, but focusing more on *how* answers are constructed could also have an impact on the complexity of their thought.

Another consideration is how we can make this kind of writing second nature. Pupils will need to practise these techniques if they are to have any hope of being able to include them in their writing repertoire. For that reason, we might design writing practice which focuses pupils on mastering technique rather than just churning out content. To that end, this sort of activity might work well:

> Read this sentence and notice the introductory word:
>
> Below, there were six birds flying carefully between rock ledges.
>
> 1. Write a sentence in which 'Above' is the introductory word.
> 2. Write a sentence in which 'Above the house' is the introductory phrase.

3. Make it a sentence describing the weather.

4. Now make it the first sentence of a ghost story.

5. Now redraft the sentence so that the phrase 'above the house' comes at the end.

6. Challenge: redraft the sentence so that the phrase 'above the house' comes in the middle, the sentence describes the weather and comes from a ghost story.[9]

What do you think? Is this kind of drill more likely to result in pupils understanding the importance of writing beautifully crafted sentences than some of the dreary, pointless story writing pupils are expected to produce?

Is grammar glamorous?

Grammar is not just a pain in the ass; it's the pole you grab to get your thoughts up on their feet and walking.

Stephen King

Well, no, it's not: grammar's that dull stuff kids got taught in the 1960s. And then enlightened educationalists decided it was unfashionable for children to know how to parse sentences and whatnot. Which leaves me part of a lost generation who trundled through our schooling without learning a blessed thing about this arcane and mysterious subject.

But it turns out that grammar really *is* an arcane and mysterious subject. Grammar and glamour come from the same root. Grammar originally meant the study of everything written but, as reading must have seemed like an almost magical skill to your average medieval peasant, grammar became synonymous with supernatural or occult knowledge. 'Grammary' came to mean magical or necromantic learning. And this leads us to 'glamour' which first meant a magical spell or

....

9   Based on ideas in Leif Fearn and Nancy Farnan, *Writing Effectively: Helping Children Master the Conventions of Writing* (Boston, MA: Allyn and Bacon, 1997), and cited by Doug Lemov on his blog post, Syntax Play: Trading Ideas with David Didau, *Doug Lemov's Field Notes* (18 October 2013). Available at: <http://teachlikeachampion.com/blog/syntax-play-trading-ideas-david-didau/>.

enchantment and has since travelled on to arrive at its modern meaning, which is about as far from the study of grammar as one could imagine.

Issues of glamour aside, pupils struggle with punctuation because they don't understand sentence structure. It's really hard to write about complex thoughts or ideas without a thorough grasp of how sentences work. And, without clear knowledge of the forms and 'rules' of writing, creativity is inevitably stifled. Ideas become a kitchen-sink soup with everything chucked into the pot with little regard for structure, audience or purpose. So, you might be asking yourself, is grammar a necessary evil or a vital component of children's writing?

My view is that children's imaginations are already pretty vast and the younger the child, the greater the depth of their imagination. We don't need to teach this, it just is. Creativity guru Sir Ken Robinson claims that children arrive in the school system with genius levels of divergent thinking.[10] Teaching is, by its nature, convergent, and by the time they reach the grand old age of 13, children have had much of their ignorance surgically removed. They've learned stuff and they know that a giant 20-foot paperclip is just silly.

By the time secondary teachers get hold of these young minds they're 11. Possibly they've already had the creative stuffing knocked out of them but, far more worryingly, they often have only the foggiest notion about word classes, sentence structure, punctuation and text organisation, not to mention spelling. What happens (and primary teachers please don't read this as blaming or passing the buck) is that word-rich pupils pick up an instinctive feel for how writing works without being able to articulate why, and everyone else doesn't.

My personal bête noire is the lie that you put a comma where you take a breath. Every single primary teacher I've ever spoken to denies imparting this arrant falsehood, but wave after wave of baffled children turn up in Year 7 with this lodged stubbornly in their brains as a known fact and not up for doubt or discussion. I've lost count of the number of pupils that I've had to disabuse of this misapprehension. It is simply not true. That said, knowing that punctuation marks were originally notation for actors on how to read scripts does give some credence to

---

10 Ken Robinson, Changing Education Paradigms [video] (2010). Available at: <http://www.ted.com/talks/ken_robinson_changing_education_paradigms.html>.

this theory. Whilst it's still fairly useful advice that you might take a breath where you *see* a comma, it's become hopelessly conflated with the instruction to writers that you put a comma wherever you take a breath. If you're asthmatic this could make for some especially interesting writing.

If creativity is the 'process of having original ideas that have value'[11] then this needs to be made distinct from mere imagination. We can think of lots of bits and bobs without actually creating anything worthwhile. This is as true of mathematics, art, music, science and engineering as it is of writing. And it's the 'having value' bit that's important here. Jotting down lots of interesting numbers but leaving out all the pesky calculations is not worthwhile. Similarly, twanging randomly at guitar strings may well give vent to your feelings but is in no way a worthwhile creation. One could perhaps argue that daubing paint randomly on canvas worked for Jackson Pollock but I (and perhaps he) might argue that he went through a rigorous process of experimentation before arriving at a new and beautiful form.

And that's the point: creation requires form. In order to write a sonnet one has to understand the rules of the sonnet form. And in order to play with the form, to experiment with the rules and, yes, to break them, you still need to know what those rules are. If you don't know how a sentence operates, how can you truly be creative in the way you construct your sentences? Just having ideas and tossing them at the page simply isn't good enough. Providing a clear, understandable framework for how to structure these ideas will actually help pupils to be more creative. They will have a greater ability to process their ideas into a form that has worth. And all this doesn't apply just to writing. Every subject has its own 'grammar' which pupils need to know before they can spread their wings and play with the tools of creation.

So we need to find ways to teach grammar creatively and sequentially that will, in turn, encourage the creativity lying dormant and unused within many of our pupils. Before we can expect pupils to use a semicolon, we need to teach them what an independent clause is. And before we can teach them about clauses, they must know about nouns and verbs.

---

11 Ken Robinson, How Schools Kill Creativity [video] 2006) Available at: <http://www.ted.com/talks/ken_robinson_says_schools_kill_creativity.html>.

Admittedly, this isn't something that needs to happen in every geography, ICT or music lesson, but it does need to happen. The best solution would be for grammar to be taught discretely, but failing that, it must be the responsibility of the English teacher.

But the problem with this is that most English teachers tend to be literature graduates. We're great at deconstructing texts and therefore tend to have a decent grasp of how to construct texts. We're less confident about language. We tend to be very comfortable discussing metaphor, alliteration and other literary techniques, but are often rather out of our depth with semicolons and conjunctions. For myself, I learned no grammar at school, and I know I'm not alone. Many younger teachers managed to avoid much in the way of formal teaching about grammar. Everything I know (and really, it's precious little) comes from having taught English as a Foreign Language (EFL) and having been forced by pupils far more knowledgeable than I about how grammar works in their native languages to explain some of the finer points of English grammar. I clung for security to my precious copy of Swan[12] and did my best to bluff it. Needless to say, if *we* don't know these things, there's little chance our pupils will!

Would it help pupils to become better writers if they knew about gerunds (a verb form used as a noun) and participles (a verb form used as an adjective)? Possibly not, but they do need to know something about how their language is constructed. Teaching grammar need not (must not, in fact) be a tedious process of rote learning. It can, and should, be every bit as active and inspired as most of what goes on in classrooms up and down the land. Why isn't it? I'd say it's because teachers are afraid of making mistakes and looking foolish.

Albert Einstein (may have) said, 'Anyone who has never made a mistake has never tried anything new.' Dylan Wiliam certainly did say, 'The best teachers fail all the time because they have such high aspirations for what their pupils can achieve.'[13] So, try something new: teach grammar creatively because real creativity does require knowledge of the rules.

---

12 Michael Swan, *Practical English Usage*, 3rd rev. edn (Oxford: Oxford University Press, 2005).

13 Wiliam, *Embedded Formative Assessment*, p. 29.

> It is an old observation that the best writers sometimes disregard the rules of rhetoric … Unless he is certain of doing as well, he will probably do best to follow the rules.[14]

The mathematics of writing

> A mathematician, like a painter or a poet, is a maker of patterns … The mathematician's patterns, like the painter's or the poet's must be beautiful; the ideas like the colours or the words, must fit together in a harmonious way. Beauty is the first test.
>
> G. H. Hardy

Could teaching grammar from the logical and precise standpoint of the mathematician be helpful?

> Grammar, like mathematics, is sequential. No one would try teaching trigonometry before teaching Pythagoras' theorem. But in English, we try dropping in a starter on colons and semi-colons in year 10 with students who have no idea about, and have probably never heard of, the independent and subordinate clause.[15]

For me, the starting point in understanding grammar is knowing that a sentence contains the following elements:

1. A subject – this is the noun (or noun phrase) which the sentence is about.

2. A verb – this is the process by which the subject interacts with the object. It is not a 'doing word'.

3. It might also contain an object – this is (usually) the noun (or noun phrase) with which the subject is interacting. Sometimes it isn't, so if you're not happy with object, refer to it as 'other'.

14 William Strunk Jr, *The Elements of Style* [ebook] (n.p.: Tribeca Books, 2011 [1918]), loc. 60–64.
15 Kirby, *How to Start on Teach First: English*, loc. 879–881.

For instance:

> I (the subject) am (the verb) a teacher (the object).

The observant among you may have noticed that I failed to label 'a' (an indefinite article) and that's deliberate. For one, I don't want to overburden anyone and also they aren't required in a sentence. A better, purer example perhaps might be:

> Jesus (subject) wept (verb).

This understanding of the subject-verb-object structure can then be applied to existing sentences:

> Like most English teachers, I'm a graduate of English literature and, like most people my age, I escaped any hint of grammar teaching in my own education.

Now, this is a fairly complex sentence made up of four different clauses, which I'll try to deconstruct into its component parts:

Subjects

Like most English teachers, I'm a graduate of English Literature and, like most people my age, I escaped any hint of grammar teaching in my own education.

Verbs

Like most English teachers, I'm a graduate of English Literature and, like most people my age, I escaped any hint of grammar teaching in my own education.

Objects

Like most English teachers, I'm a graduate of English Literature and, like most people my age, I escaped any hint of grammar teaching in my own education.

And other stuff:

Conjunction

Like most English teachers, I'm a graduate of English Literature and, like most people my age, I escaped any hint of grammar teaching in my own education.

Preposition	Noun phrase	Conjunction
	(in this case an object)	

If you were then to transcribe this sentence as part of an equation it would look something like this:

P O, S V O C, P O, S V O

The commas are doing a similar job to that of + signs and help us see the different clauses within the sentence.

This is useful when marking pupils' writing and you come across something like this:

As I ran down the street.

Because it starts with 'As' (a coordinating conjunction) it's a subordinate clause and cannot therefore be a sentence in and of itself. Our response to this fragment (unfinished sentence) is to scream, 'What? What happened when you ran down the street?' Pupils need to know that where this happens a sentence needs to look like this:

As I ran down the street, I tripped.

C S V O, S V

Or

As I ran down the street, I headbutted an old person.

C S V O, S V O

Anything that is left merely as C S V O is wrong.

It's also worth knowing that if a subordinate clause begins a sentence it is always followed by a comma, so that, in effect, you would be leaving the comma dangling and then just starting a new sentence with a capital letter. Obviously, you wouldn't do that because the vast majority of people know that you end a sentence with a full stop. But what if commas were understood in the same way? What if we knew, deep in our souls, that you only ever use a comma to divide single items (nouns or adjectives, or phrases if you want to get technical) in a list or when a subordinate clause begins or is embedded in a sentence?

If we knew that, we could teach it. If we knew that a sentence describes the relationship between a subject and its object then maybe we'd have more luck communicating this knowledge to our pupils.

We could then instruct them to write a sentence that did this:

S V O; S V O

Or this:

V, S O

And, by God, they'd know how to do it!

But language is messy. Maths, on the other hand, is neat and ordered. If algebra makes sense to you, it is because it is a realm of certainties. So, can writing harness some of this logic and precision (whilst remaining mindful that 'fiction that does nothing but follow rules is cold arithmetic'[16])? Can we give pupils the mental tools to be able to construct technically accurate sentences? And does it even matter?

Some may argue that all this emphasis on grammar stifles creativity. To them I say, pah! We wouldn't value a mathematician so focused on a creative solution to a problem that they couldn't add up, or an architect whose 'creative' buildings were unbuildable. We value precision in so many other fields, why is it OK for writing to be sloppy?

I'm pleased to report that after eight weeks of an intensive crash course in grammar, my AS class are now able to write. They are so much more thoughtful about how they're writing rather than just dumping their thoughts on the page. I would argue, and so would they, that this has allowed them to be much more confident and creative in their writing. Most of all, it's allowed them to decide when, where and why they might want to break the rules.

And crucially, none of this need be dull. Just as there are bucket loads of creative, exciting maths teachers out there, so too can there be regiments of outstanding grammarians.

---

16 Godfrey H. Hardy, *A Mathematician's Apology* (Cambridge: Cambridge University Press, 1941), quoted in Istvan Banyai, Why Writers Should Learn Math, *The New Yorker* (2 November 2012). Available at: <http://www.newyorker.com/online/blogs/books/2012/11/writers-should-learn-math.html>

Building vocabulary

The limits of my language mean the limits of my world.

Ludwig Wittgenstein

Our vocabulary has an enormous impact on our experience of the world. Not only does it open doors to new ideas, it enriches our thinking and, after physical attractiveness, is the determining factor behind our choice of friends and partners. As we saw in Chapter 1, at the age of 7, word-rich children know an average of 7,000 words whereas word-poor children only know about 3,000 words. And, because of the Matthew Effect, this gap only widens over time. In order to close this gap we need to find some way to increase word-poor pupils' vocabulary.

It's widely believed that the best way to build pupils' vocabulary is through context via 'wide reading'. The thinking goes that if pupils read widely enough they will encounter lots of new words and be able to infer their meaning through the context in which they find them. Now, there's nothing wrong with wide reading and, of course, this is something we want to encourage. But, if we make the mistake of believing that this is the best way to build vocabulary, we are sadly mistaken.

When we come across new words in conversation with others, the context is usually clear, but when we run into a new word in a text there is the problem that in written contexts there is no intonation, body language or shared physical surroundings to support learning new words. Written language is a far less effective medium for building vocabulary than spoken language. Typically, pupils only learn between five and fifteen of every 100 new words encountered in written texts.[17]

And this isn't the only problem. Word-poor children are also far less likely to read widely than their word-rich peers. So, on the rare occasions they stumble upon new vocabulary, they'll be very unlikely to learn much of it. Relying on naturally occurring text to build vocabulary will only result in the gap widening.

The solution is to teach vocabulary directly. Now, obviously, there's no way you can teach every kid all the words they're ever going to need. Thankfully, we don't have

17 Isabel Beck, Margaret McKeown and Linda Kucan, *Bringing Words to Life: Robust Vocabulary Instruction*, 2nd edn (New York: Guilford Press, 2013), p. 5.

to. Many words occur so frequently that there's no need to teach them. These are 'everyday' words that are likely to be used in informal conversations. Others are the subject-specific preserve of academic disciplines and will naturally be taught whenever the need arises. No science teacher would neglect to teach the meaning of *osmosis*, just as no geographer would omit defining *meander*. We can feel confident that as they arise, words like *sonnet*, *isotope* and *phoneme* will be explained. The problem arises with those words which occupy the space between these two extremes. These are words which are unlikely to occur in conversation but which are quite likely to turn up in a wide range of written texts – words such as *contradict*, *miscellaneous*, *intrinsic*, *harbinger*, *surmise* and *predetermine*.[18] Making sure pupils know and can use these words would make an enormous difference to their chances of being academically successful, but would this be a reasonable use of our limited time? Beck et al. estimate that there are about 7,000 word families which fall into this category of words which occur in a wide range of written texts.[19] Even if we decided to teach only half of these, how on earth would we find the time?

Well, as individual teachers, we can't. This is a programme on which a school might embark but it is beyond the reach or control of individuals. We can, however, give pupils strategies for learning new words based on knowledge of the morphemes from which words are constructed. Loads of words in the English language are derived from Greek and Latin roots. Knowing these roots helps us to grasp the meaning of words before we look them up in the dictionary. It also helps us to see how words are often arranged in families with similar characteristics. English teacher Joe Kirby suggests that instead of teaching words, we should teach the roots from which they're formed. In that way, instead of just teaching one word, we're potentially teaching hundreds of words.

....

18 Beck et al. refer to these words as 'Tier Two' words: *Bringing Words to Life*, pp. 9–10.

19 Beck et al., *Bringing Words to Life*, p. 10.

And, generously, he's provided a list of the most frequently used roots for use in our lessons:

Greek and Latin roots

Meaning	Examples
re – again, back	reuse, refill, reconnect, recycle, review, revisit, rewind, rebound, react
mis, dis, un – not (opposite, reverse)	misplace, misinform, dishonest, disorganised, disobey, dismount, disappear, unfriendly, untie, unlock,
ex – out	exit, exclaim, exhaust, exhilarate, excavate, exhume, export, extravagant, extraordinary
pre, pro – before	previous, preliminary, predict, prepare, precede, previous, precaution, prevaricate, premature, preamble, prelude, proponent, proceed, propose, prodigy, prototype
inter – among	international, interrupt, internship, interject, interview, interstate, interrogate, interfere, intercept
bene – good	benefit, beneficial, benevolent, benefactor
sub – under	subtract, submerge, submarine, subdue, subjugate
post – after	post-war, postpone, postgraduate, posterity, posthumous
super – over	supreme, superficial, superlative, supersede
mono – single	monologue, monarch, monopoly, monochrome, monocle, monosyllabic, monotheistic
sequer – after	sequel, sequence, subsequent, consecutive, sequential, non sequitur
poly – many	polygon, polytheistic, polyglot, polysyllabic
primus – first	primary, primitive, primeval, primer

contra – against	contrary, contradict, counterproductive, contraband
medius – middle	medium, mediate, mediocre, mediocrity, intermediate, media
vita – life	vitamin, vitality, revitalise, vital
amo – love	amiable, amorous, enamoured
specto – look	inspect, speculate, perspective, spectre, spectrograph
caput – head	cap, captain, decapitate, capitulate, capsize, caption
fido – trust	confide, confidential, fidelity, infidel, infidelity
pan – all	panorama, panacea, panel, pantheon, pan-African
circum – around	circumscribe, circumvent, circulate, circumference
copio – plenty	copious, copy, cornucopia
hyper – over	hyperactive, hyperventilate, hypercritical, hypersensitive, hypertension
brevis – short	brief, brevity, abbreviate
occido – kill	suicide, homicide, matricide, infanticide, regicide, fratricide
culpa – blame	culprit, culpable, culpability
hypo – under	hypochondriac, hypothermic, hypoglycaemic
malus – bad	malevolent, malice, malicious, malady, malefactor, malodorous, malapropism
ter/terr – earth	territory, extraterrestrial
tele – far	telephone, television
vac – empty	vacant, vacuum, evacuate
log, logue – word, thought, speech	monologue, astrology, biology, neologism

dic, dict – to speak	dictionary, dictator

Source: Adapted from Joe Kirby, *How to Start on Teach First: English* [Kindle edn]
(London: Teach First), loc. 860–862.

It's also worth teaching pupils prefixes and suffixes. Knowing the Greek and Latin roots of several prefixes and suffixes can also help us determine the meaning of words. *Ante*, for instance, means before, and if we connect *bellum* with belliger-ent to work out the connection with war, we'll know that antebellum refers to a period before war. Useful common prefixes include:

- Quantity: semi, uni, mono, bi, di, cent, kilo, mili

- Negation: a, il, in ir un, anti, counter, de, dis, mis

- Time: ante, fore, pre, pro, post, re

- Direction or position: super, trans, infra, sub, hypo, pro, pre, re, ex, in, im, en, em, circum, peri

Suffixes, on the other hand, modify the meaning of a word and often deter-mine what it's doing in a sentence. Take the noun 'nation', for example. With suffixes, the word becomes the adjective 'national', the adverb 'nationally', and the verb 'nationalise'.

See what words you can come up with that use the following suffixes:

- Noun suffixes: -ence, -ance, -or, -er, -ment, -ist, -ism, -ship, -ency, -sion, -tion, -ness, -hood, -dom

- Verb suffixes: -en, -ify, -ise, -ate

- Adjective suffixes: -able, -ible, -al, -ial, -tic, -ly, -ful, -ous, -ive, -less, -ish, -ulent

- The adverb suffix is -ly (although not all words that end in -ly are adverbs, like friendly)

Armed with this body of knowledge, pupils will be far better equipped to puzzle out the meanings of words they meet in context, but there will still be times when they'll be stumped because contexts are often misleading.

Here are some illustrations of what can go wrong.

Misdirective contexts

Consider this extract:

> Antonia considered her investment portfolio. She had a great deal of ready cash, several investment properties, and any number of stocks and bonds. Knowing how much money she'd made last year, she was anticipating a *ghastly* meeting with the Inland Revenue.

If you didn't know what *ghastly* meant, what would you infer from the context? Antonia seems to be doing pretty well, which would lead us to believe that ghastly must mean something positive. The context actively points us in the wrong direction and makes it impossible to work out the meaning of the word.

Nondirective contexts

Whilst nondirective contexts are not actively unhelpful, they don't actually give us any clues:

> The girls talked about last weekend's party discussing each of the guests in turn. When they got on to the subject of Christopher, they agreed that he was the most *gregarious* person they knew.

Here we have no idea what *gregarious* might mean. We don't know whether Christopher is considered positively or negatively. There are no clues on which to fix a meaning.

General contexts

General contexts allow readers to get the gist of new words without being able to pinpoint a specific meaning:

The dark woods were full of *sinister* noises.

We can infer from this extract that dark woods are likely to contain things which might be scary or unpleasant. Therefore, we can approximate the meaning of *sinister* as being generally negative without being precisely clear of its exact definition.

Directive contexts

And then sometimes there are directive contexts which make it reasonably straightforward to work out what unfamiliar words mean:

Albert had worked really hard on preparing his report. Everyone was so impressed that they applauded and complimented him throughout the hour-long meeting. It was obvious that he enjoyed their *fulsome* praise.

Here we can work out that Albert has made a real effort on something and then basked in the congratulations of his colleagues. Since they've made such a fuss of him, we can be fairly certain that *fulsome* praise must mean a lot of praise, or enthusiastic praise.

But this doesn't happen intentionally. Writers don't set out to make the meanings of words clear to their readers. They expect us to understand *effusive* as fully as *gregarious* or *ghastly*, and to be able to follow their thoughts and ideas. It is only through having this understanding that we can deduce that Antonia is dreading her meeting and that possibly the girls fancy Christopher.

So, what does this mean? Well, firstly it tells us that we shouldn't assume pupils will acquire vocabulary through context. In fact, we should assume that they won't.

This being the case, we need to actively teach the vocabulary pupils will need to access the texts we give them to read. We can do this in several different ways:

1. Read through any texts you intend to use in advance, making a note of the 'tractors (see page 115) and deciding how to introduce this vocabulary before the text is read.

2. Read the text with pupils and teach unfamiliar words as you go.

3. Ask pupils themselves to highlight words they don't recognise and then spend time explaining these words before asking pupils to re-read.

The first option is the most time consuming in terms of planning but is likely to lead to the best outcome for word-poor pupils. As ever, weary teachers have to decide where best they will expend their limited resources.

However we identify them, what should we do when we come across these pesky Tier Two words? Well, possibly the worst thing to do is to rely on getting kids to look words up in dictionaries. It's not just that dictionary work is dull, it's more that dictionary definitions are often so opaque that they leave pupils none the wiser. Here are a few suggestions on what might be a more effective approach:

- Give examples of specific circumstances in which the word might be used: 'You might use the word *heave* when you lift something that's very heavy.'
- Give examples in everyday language: 'Someone who is *persuasive* can talk other people into doing things.'

We can also take the opportunity to deliberately introduce Tier Two words:

- If the text is about a dirty dog, we could introduce the word *soiled*.
- If the text refers to an island that is far from civilization, we can introduce the word *remote*.
- If a character in a story doesn't like to spend money, we could introduce the words *parsimonious* or *miserly*.

And finally, some general principles for teaching vocabulary:

- Teach students to relate words to their existing background knowledge.

- Teach new words in relation to known words.

- Teach words systematically and in depth.

- Give multiple opportunities for word use: pre-reading, during reading, post reading and in subsequent lessons.

- Awaken an interest in, and enthusiasm for, words.

Chapter 7
How written feedback and marking can support literacy

Marking is an act of love.

Phil Beadle

What's the point of marking?

If you've never taken part in a whole-school book scrutiny, I'd recommend doing so. Seeing how pupils treat their exercise books across different subjects is very revealing. I'll happily agree that exercise books can never give a complete picture of pupils' learning and progress in particular classes, but they certainly raise interesting questions about whether marking and presentation matter. And they give a pretty clear indication of whether feedback is having an impact on pupils' progress.

As an aside, try running an INSET day where teachers scrutinise each other's books. This may sound heartless and unfair, but isn't this a matter of professional pride? And if not, just as pupils need to know I'll be looking at their work, I need to know that someone else will be looking at my marking.

In what has become folklore at a school I worked in, one teacher said to another after they had been given an opportunity to observe each other, 'You're the reason SLT give us a hard time!' A decent leader should have a damned good idea as to

whose books need monitoring and whose can be used as exemplars. Middle leaders should be scrutinising their team's books regularly and sharing the findings in a non-judgemental way, but a way which is very clear about their high expectations. This is just too important to leave to chance.

Have you ever flicked back through an exercise book and seen the same repeated comments followed, with soul-numbing certainty, by the same repeated mistakes? There are few things more crushing to the spirit of hardworking teachers than this dramatically enacted evidence that, apparently, most of the feedback given by teachers to pupils falls on stony soil because pupils find it confusing, non-reasoned and not understandable![1] A damning triumvirate! And even when pupils *think they understand* the feedback we give them, they don't really know what to do with it.

Just for a moment, let's assume we all understand and agree that giving quality feedback to pupils can have more impact on pupils' progress than pretty much anything else teachers can do. Let's also assume we agree that whilst other forms of feedback may be equally valuable, teachers marking books is one of the most important and effective ways of ensuring that pupils are getting clear, timely feedback on how well they are making progress. This being the case, why do we waste so much time on distractions which have little or no impact?

Phil Beadle, in typically provocative style, puts it like this:

> You can turn up hungover every morning, wearing the same creased pair of Farahs as last week, with hair that looks like a bird has slept in it, then spend most of the lesson talking at kids about how wonderful you are; but mark their books with dedication and rigour and your class will fly.[2]

Not only does this make me feel slightly better about my weakness for Pinot Noir, it also confirms what I've long believed: the more often I mark their books, the more effort they will put into their work. No effort on my part = no effort on theirs.

....

1 Hattie, *Visible Learning for Teachers*, p. 122.

2 Beadle, *How to Teach*, p. 213.

Marking is one of those things that most teachers feel perennially guilty about. There's always something to mark, and when you're tired and stressed it's often the first thing to go. But over the past few years, the thing that has improved most in my teaching is without doubt my marking. What was once an endless, dreaded millstone hanging around my guilty neck has been transformed from chore to, if not a pleasure, certainly a highlight of my working routine. Now, I keenly anticipate their eager little faces reading through my carefully crafted instructions on how to improve. Gone is the meaningless empty praise of 'Well done!' and gone too is the time spent fruitlessly scratching about for some meaningless platitude that I'm pretty sure will never make the slightest dent in pupils' almost willful determination to misuse apostrophes and omit capital letters.

Directed Improvement and Reflection Time

The big difference, for me, is DIRT. The idea that I should dedicate part or all of a lesson to Directed Improvement and Reflection Time in which pupils act on my feedback has been a revelation. All those hours spent marking now have a visible impact. I tell them how to improve and, by God, they do it. There's no trick to it, no gimmick, nothing clever or mysterious – just the embedded routine of high expectations. The advantages are twofold: every pupil has an individual lesson plan based on your careful marking, and they get to consolidate their learning and have an opportunity to master the skills and knowledge that have been studied.

Clevedon School's response to DIRT is Triple Impact Marking. The three figures below show how this works in English (other subjects should adapt it as appropriate):

TIM in English

Step one – you will:

- Use the CSP Code to proofread your work
- Highlight work you are proud of
- Explain how you have met the Success Criteria

Clevedon School English department marking policy I

TIM in English

Step two – your teacher will:

- Use the CSP Code to point out your mistakes
- Use the Success Criteria to explain how you can improve
- Set specific tasks for you to complete

Clevedon School English department marking policy II

TIM in English

Step three – you will:

- Read the feedback written in books
- Answer any questions the teacher has asked
- Complete the tasks the teacher has set

Clevedon School English department marking policy III

Neat, eh? But don't fall into the trap of thinking that just because you've put a system like this in place, that pupils will automatically act on your feedback. Here's an example of what can go wrong:

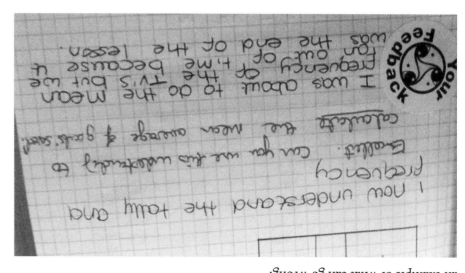

DIRT: What we want to avoid

In the example above, the pupil has wasted time explaining why they haven't acted on feedback instead of actually doing it! This serves to demonstrate that no system is foolproof and that pupils will find ways to confound your expectations. DIRT needs embedding and pupils will need to practise acting on feedback before they get good at it.

OK, so you're using DIRT. Good for you. Here are a few of my thoughts on some of the other principles that underlie effective and efficient marking.

Dialogue

A pupil's exercise book can be an almost sacred space in which a teacher can gently prod their charges from ignorant caterpillars into the iridescence of knowledge and understanding. One of the many changes I've made to my marking practice is

to encourage pupils to 'talk' to me via their books. Instead of making comments, I now ask questions: Why have you done …? How could you improve …? Is … correct? And, in return, they can ask their own questions, make points of information or clarify my misunderstandings and assumptions. Some of what they have to say is profound and some is sometimes witlessly banal. But I always try to respond. I've experimented with asking them to write these conversational gambits in particular coloured pens or to use designated parts of the page, but I've settled on a mostly freestyle dialogue that unfolds when and if pupils feel they need or want it. But, because lessons are constructed around giving and responding to feedback, these conversations take place far more than they ever did when I left to pupils' ad hoc whimsy. For the record, I'm not a fan of WWW (What Went Well)/EBI (Even Better If) – it just doesn't seem to generate a dialogue.

Find faults and fix

I also give lessons over to making sure that work is well presented. In the past, this wasn't something I cared about all that much but reading Ron Berger's *An Ethic of Excellence* changed all that.[3] I now embrace his claim that if it isn't perfect, it isn't finished.' Of course, the confines of classrooms and curriculums mean that there just isn't enough time to achieve perfection, but that doesn't mean we shouldn't aim for it. I often direct pupils to find faults and fix them just before I collect the books in. This means that the basics all have to be in place – neatly underlined titles and dates and so on – but there is also an expectation that pupils will proof-read their work. My rule is that if they fail to proofread, I won't mark it. Sounds draconian, but it works. The same is true of sloppy work. In the past, I'd often noticed a trend where the quality of presentation sharply deteriorated a few weeks after a new book was issued. Now, when kids hand in work which is clearly below their best levels of presentation, I make them write it out again. You rarely have to do this more than once before the message sinks in: you should be proud of your work, and that includes its presentation.

3 Ron Berger, *An Ethic of Excellence: Building a Culture of Craftsmanship with Students* (Portsmouth, NH: Heinemann Educational Books, 2003).

Marking is planning

If I'm going to commit time to marking a set of books, I want that to be time I don't have to spend planning lesson activities. Now, because of DIRT, the marking is the activity. For younger children, 10–15 minutes of a lesson might be usefully spent improving work and acting on feedback, but for older children, I can easily get one or more lessons out of my marking. The more questions I ask and the more tasks I set, the more time they will be expected to spend in response. Dylan Wiliam says that feedback should be more work for the recipient than the donor, and he's right. If it's taken me a minute to mark a piece of work, that should result in 10 minutes worth of improvement.

Marking is differentiation

Marking is the purest form of differentiation. There can be no better way to respond to the needs of an individual than to read what they have written and give them specific tasks to challenge them to be better than they currently are. In an ideal world, I would mark their books after every piece of written work and give each pupil detailed and individual feedback for them to act on during the following lesson: pupils do work, I mark it with feedback that requires them to do (or re-do) something and then they do it. Based on my knowledge of each individual, I will have a good idea of what they're capable of and whether the work they've handed in demonstrates progress. And, pleasingly, every pupil in the class has a uniquely differentiated lesson plan.

Time is precious

Despite all the juice I try to squeeze out of my marking, there's always scope to save more time. I love Lisa Ashes's idea of using + − = to mark.[4] Here's my take on it. At the beginning of a new topic or unit of work, teachers' feedback needs to be very precise and detailed (as well as being clearly labelled). Then, all subsequent marking on redrafted work can just be given a +, − or = sign so pupils must look back at their written feedback to work out why and how they will go about improving.

Joe Kirby has also written about how using symbols can save precious time:

Don't write out comments. You end up writing such similar comments across the class, and they won't read them anyway.

Instead, get them to write them out. Choose three to five targets or questions before you start marking, then scan their answer, choose the best fit between the student's work and the group target, and draw an icon. One minute per book maximum. At the start of the next lesson, you write the targets on the board, students write their targets in their books. They get instant feedback and can take action on their target straight away.[5]

Another favourite time-saving technique is to focus your marking on what will really make an impact. What if, instead of marking everything, we only marked the bits where pupils are struggling, where they've made particularly telling mistakes or where they've really taken a risk? But surely it's impossible to find these rare nuggets without wading through the whole darn thing? The solution is to ask pupils to highlight those areas where they really want feedback. Ask them where they struggled or where they've taken a risk – they'll generally know right away which parts they're most anxious about and this means you can home in on the most crucial aspects of their work without burning out.

4   See Lisa Ashes's blog post: ASSESS Keep it Simple Plus – Minus – Equals, *The Learning Geek* (29 August 2013). Available at: <http://thelearninggeek.com/2013/08/assess-keep-it-simple-plus-minus-equals/>.

5   See Joe Kirby's blog post: How Can I Mark Books Without Burning Out?, *Back to the Whiteboard* (22 June 2012). Available at: <http://back2thewhiteboard.wordpress.com/2012/06/22/5-how-can-i-mark-books-without-burning-out/>

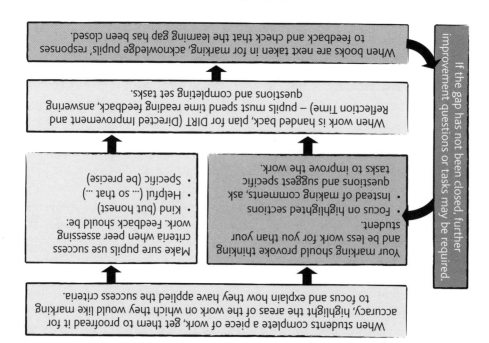

Feedback flowchart

Presentation and drafting

It's an inspiration to know that 'beautiful work' is not just possible but actively worth pursuing. Lack of time may not allow us to achieve perfection, but we should certainly aim for quality. We need to explain why sloppy work is unacceptable. If you want titles underlined, get pupils to think about the reasons and explain what the point might be; don't just insist on compliance. They will not value their written work unless we do. I suggest regular amnesty lessons to ensure books are up to snuff; get pupils to go back over their work looking for errors and correcting them and insist they take pride in what they produce.

I have started referring to writing as 'drafting', as in: 'I want you to draft an article on ...' This then encourages redrafting. My thinking is that if pupils know from

the outset that this is how writing is supposed to work then maybe they will see more point in moving towards a beautiful, finely crafted end product. But none of this will happen unless they know, deep down in their souls, that I will be checking.

Easy for me to say? As an English teacher I have fewer classes than, say, your average humanities teacher. How on earth are they supposed to keep up with this workload? I'd tentatively suggest that marking once every four lessons is a reasonable ratio. This would mean that core subjects mark once a week and RE teachers don't get too swamped. Obviously, this isn't always going to feel possible and there should be some leeway built in. But setting aside an hour a day for marking is time well spent. And as you get used to it, the more efficient you'll become.

Of course, this is not easy. If you have 15+ classes a week you're really going to struggle to look at their books often enough to make a difference to their learning. But that's the issue, isn't it? Just covering content won't cut it and, other than redesigning your curriculum to avoid this kind of logjam, the only way forward is to set up a system whereby pupils do the majority of lesson-to-lesson monitoring and critique and you put together a timetable to mark each class's books once per term. I know this is a tough gig, but if you approach marking as planning then it might seem a little more do-able.

I glibly repeated this mantra that 'marking is planning' in a meeting recently, only to be bluntly told that this is not the case in science. Now, I've nothing against science teachers or science lessons, but I just don't see this. Of course I appreciate that science teachers are under enormous pressure to cover content, but surely not at the expense of making sure that children have learned what has already been taught? Of course, subjects are different, and what works in my English lesson won't necessarily work in the same way in science, but unless you mark their books how on earth will you know whether what you're teaching is having any effect? Yes, you can use traffic lights, hinge questions, exit cards and other Assessment for Learning (AfL) paraphernalia to get a sense of pupils' understanding, but there's nothing like trial by extended answer for separating the knows from the know-nots. Maybe this was a misunderstanding. Maybe we understood different things by 'marking'. Dylan Wiliam has observed that in most English speaking countries teachers spend much more time alone, marking, than teachers in, say,

Japan. Instead of marking, Japanese teachers spend a big chunk of their 'lesson preparation time working together to devise questions to use in order to find out whether their teaching has been successful.'[6]

This is fascinating and begs a couple of questions. Firstly, should we mark our books alone? And secondly, what if marking was concerned with devising questions to find out whether teaching has been successful? On the first question, I'm all for marking collaboratively and, of course, moderation and standardisation are vital. Sadly, it just isn't practical to do this all the time. Much as I love the teachers in my department, I really don't want to spend that much time with them! But having some sort of 'marking buddy' with whom we regularly compare our books is probably a healthy and sensible thing to do.

The second question takes us back to DIRT. The type of marking I'm advocating, and that I'd hope to see in pupils' books, should lead to thoughtful, dialogic questions based on the work pupils have done and be designed to prompt them to make progress.

6   Dylan Wiliam, Keeping Learning on Track: Formative Assessment and the Regulation of Learning. In M. Coupland, J. Anderson and T. Spencer (eds), *Making Mathematics Vital: Proceedings of the Twentieth Biennial Conference of the Australian Association of Mathematics Teachers* (Adelaide: Australian Association of Mathematics Teachers Inc., 2007), p. 22.

The problem with peer assessment

Hey! Nice haircut.
Your face is a bit repellent.
But your dress is beautiful.

The praise sandwich

So, how much of the feedback that pupils get do you think comes from their peers? I'm not talking about feedback on their choice of trainers or on their ability to wear a hoodie with dash and élan; I'm talking about classroom feedback on their learning.

So, go on, how much? When asked to guess, most teachers hazard something along the lines of 10–20%. In fact, according to research undertaken by Graham Nuthall, the actual figure is more like 80%. And of that, 80% is, apparently, wrong.[7]

This leaves us with something of a problem. Whether we encourage it or not, whether were aware of it or not, pupils are giving each other erroneous feedback on their work continually. If this alarms you as much as it does me, we have a limited number of choices. We can either make them work in absolute silence and

7   Cited in Hattie, Visible Learning for Teachers, p. 131.

stand over them with a rolled-up newspaper ready to beat the slightest misappre-hension into submission or we can try to harness the prevalence of peer feedback and work to improve its accuracy. We can, of course, do neither of these things, but that would result in perpetuating an awful lot of misinformation and misun-derstanding and, on balance, I cannot recommend this.

And even when pupils' feedback isn't wrong, it can be pretty bland and meaning-less. We've all suffered from peer assessment which has generated such priceless gems as 'make it neater' and 'do more', which, whilst possibly helpful, will have zero impact on their luckless chum's ability to improve. Clearly, we can give them clear, focused success criteria to inform their feedback, but whilst this may mean they make better comments in formal peer assessment, it has little traction on all the informal feedback flying around.

My point is that although this may be the case in some classrooms, it doesn't have to be in mine. Peer assessment has long been a vaunted component of AfL, with the intention being that pupils should be 'activated as learning resources for one another'.[8] I've been as guilty as anyone in the past of getting pupils to mindlessly dribble about 'what went well' and 'how work could have been better even if …' Clearly, well-designed success criteria are essential for this process to be effective, but even more important is that the process is public and transparent. If pupils know that you and everyone else are going to be reading their scrawled, 'Great work LOL!!! – maybe do a bit more next time :)', and that it will be held up as unacceptable, then maybe they'll think a little more about how their feedback can be formative.

Well, I can heartily recommend American educator Ron Berger's impassioned plea for 'beautiful work', *An Ethic of Excellence*. In it he lays out his manifesto for creating a culture of craftsmanship in schools, part of which is his insistence that if work isn't perfect, it isn't finished.[9] A big part of this is that pupils need to get used to drafting and redrafting their work alongside regular public critique ses-sions in which they offer each other advice and guidance on how to improve their work. Berger explains that if pupils are trained in the protocols of critique, they

---

8 Wiliam, *Embedded Formative Assessment*, p. 46.

9 Berger, *An Ethic of Excellence*, p. 99.

will be able to offer each other informal feedback which allows them to improve dramatically.[10]

Not only is this great for demonstrating progress and encouraging resilience, it can have a huge impact on pupils' ability to give each other feedback which is useful.

Berger outlines a number of principles essential for getting the critique process right:

1. Feedback should be kind, helpful and specific.
2. It should be hard on content but soft on people.
3. All pupils need the opportunity to step up and share their thoughts and then step back and let others have their turn.

Critique protocols

Being a tinkerer by nature, I can never just leave these ideas entirely alone and have polluted the purity of Ron's message with the following advice.

Kind

It's all very well for feedback to be kind but this is something most pupils are already a bit too comfortable with. They will happily festoon their feedback with smiley faces, kisses and other mitigations, all of which ensure that they're so busy being inoffensive that nothing of value gets said. So feedback needs to be kind, but honest and this can be achieved by focusing on the work, not on the pupil. They should depersonalise their comments by avoiding statements like 'You haven't ...' and rephrasing as, 'It should have ...' Also, phrasing advice in the form of a question can make it much easier to hear and then act on.

10 I would also recommend watching Berger explain critique in this short video: <http://howtovideos.hightechhigh.org/video/275/Ron+Berger+on+Critique+part+2+of+2>.

Helpful

I'm very keen on teachers (and pupils) explaining why our instructions should be acted on. To this end, I've found it helpful to insist that pupils should take the trouble to explain why their advice is helpful by adding a 'so that …' onto whatever it was they were suggesting. This might result in a comment along the lines of 'Begin the first sentence with an adverb so that it makes it more impact and your sentences are more varied.' This idea is synthesised (pinched) from Zoë Elder's advice on using the phrase 'so that'[11] to construct learning outcomes that provide a link between what pupils are learning and the reason they're learning it.

Specific

The more precise feedback is, the easier it is to act on. I tell pupils to zoom in on details and offer specific advice for improving these. They should be making suggestions along the lines of 'Can you think of some alternatives for the word "weird"? or Can you think of something else the writer might have meant by the word "cold"?' When feedback is as specific as this it's almost impossible not to act on it.

This all requires effort. Embedding a culture where pupils give each other high quality feedback informally will not happen by itself or because you wish it were so. In my limited experience, I've found that some groups are better at it than others but all groups require persistence to get it right.

The start of the journey is to use guided critique sessions. In these, I model the critique process by focusing on a small number of pupils and encouraging all members of the class to 'step up' to offer critique and 'step back' so that everyone gets a say. This is vital if you want to build affiliation within your classroom and it makes the process safe. Most importantly, as a teacher, I can

----

11 See Zoë Elder's blog post: Constructing Learning SO THAT it is Meaningful and Purposeful, *Full On Learning* (1 October 2012). Available at: <http://fullonlearning.com/2012/10/01/constructing-learning-so-that-it-is-meaningful-and-purposeful/>.

also engage in meta-critique by discussing whether comments are conforming to the critique protocols.

Gallery critique

From critique protocols, we should aim to use gallery critique sessions. This is where everyone (including the teacher) lays out their drafts for each other to look at and spends a lesson, or part of a lesson, commenting kindly, helpfully and specifically on each other's work. I've found that it pays to give pupils a fair bit of warning about these sessions as displaying their work before they're ready can be damaging for some of the more fragile egos in your class. But the benefit is immense: most pupils immediately begin to take more pride in their work when they know the whole class will be scrutinising it. I've had some pupils who are reluctant to take part in the process at first, so I've found it easier to let them wait until they see the benefits. It's normally at the second gallery critique session that the progress of some becomes truly evident. Those who haven't been trying or who feel ashamed of what they've produced start to see the point in making the effort and learn to see that making mistakes is just part of the process of creating beautiful work. For any kind of written work, I would heartily recommend that Slow Writing (see pages 161–165) be part of this process.

Example of gallery critique from an AS English language lesson

In the example, the critique offered on the sticky note in the centre is particularly helpful. It reads:

Very well organised. Are you sure you don't want to use specific terminology? Would it not make sense in context? What is the purpose? What do you want readers to feel?

Phrasing the critique as questions is a great way to get peers to act on suggestions, as it feels less direct and pointed than a statement. Also, it's more likely to provoke thought and consideration.

The final stage, and the point at which we all want to end up, is the point at which critique becomes informal. I start to embed this by asking a class to offer each other critique at various points during the lesson and float around monitoring that all is well. Eventually, if you persevere, you'll be rewarded by hearing this happening without you directing it. These are the golden moments for which we teach, and some of my classes have become wonderful at supporting each other through the process of mastering skills and creating high quality products.

Like most great teaching, this is incredibly simple, but it ain't easy. You will get it wrong along the way and, if you're anything like me, some of your mistakes will be spectacular. But, if you believe it's worth doing, if you persevere and if you're determined, it will pay dividends.

Potential pitfalls

Here's an FAQ on some of the questions I field from teachers anxious to avoid the pitfalls inherent in trying to embed a culture of critique:

Q: How do you manage a mixed-ability class where less able pupils are expected to critique more able pupils' work?

A: Manage gallery critique so that the weakest pupils do the rounds with you as teacher's assistants; point out to them how and why you're critiquing, concentrate on those pupils whose work is 'just out of reach' and explain how they might emulate it. Others might need critique stems to help them make meaningful comments. I sometimes give out pro formas; sometimes I focus them on the Thought Stems on my classroom wall. In more informal critique sessions it

all depends on your seating plan; think carefully about selecting critique partners whom pupils will benefit from working with.

Q: What happens with poorly behaved, demotivated pupils? How do you make
them take part and not ruin it for others?

A: I don't. I encourage them to take part, of course, but I wait for them to be ready.
In my Year 9 class I initially had three reluctant class members who wouldn't
share their work and weren't prepared to 'step up' to offer kind, helpful and specific critique. (It's important to come down hard on anyone deliberately offering
critique which does not meet these requirements.) As a class we picked them
off one by one; they quickly started to see the benefits and felt they were very
much on the outside of the classroom culture we were establishing. One boy
took two months before he started to give way and still has times when he
chooses not to take part, but this is so much better than he might have been in
a different classroom environment.

Q: Some higher ability pupils struggle to accept feedback from their peers – how
would you approach this?

A: By making your own work part of the critique process. Model accepting criticism and acting on feedback. Also, sometimes it's helpful to reword pupils' critique so that it's more understandable and easier to accept. Normally, pupils
refuse to act on feedback when it's perceived as not kind enough or not helpful
enough. Make sure comments are 'soft on people' and that the 'so that …' has
been clearly articulated – without this some may not see the point. Sometimes
it's our job to help bridge the communication gap by rewording and smoothing.
We also need to be aware of pupils with fixed mindsets and help them to take
a more 'growth mindset' approach to feedback.

Q: What happens when a pupil has 'done everything' and other pupils can't think
of any feedback to move them on?

A: Ha! That old chestnut! Normally this is my fault because I won't have pitched
the work high enough and my success criteria might not be clear enough.
Remember, pupils need to be challenged. As long as they're supported appropriately any pupil can learn anything. Our job is to give our classes difficult things
to do and then provide sufficient scaffolding for them to be able to get on with
it. And then I ask them to work out how we can make more interesting mistakes.
Works a treat.

But also, we need to make the success criteria absolutely clear so that peers can
give kind, specific and useful feedback. One way to do this is to design the success criteria with pupils so that they have some ownership of them.

Last words

So there it is: all my advice on improving reading, writing and oracy across the curriculum.

The key messages with which I'd like to leave you are:

Start with why – explain why literacy is so important

There's a whole host of reasons why it's important to be literate, not least the fact that the digital world has made reading and writing even more central to our lives than ever before. But remember the Matthew Effect. If we don't take every opportunity to actively teach academic language through our subjects then we are ensuring that the gap between the word-rich and the word-poor persists.

Make the implicit explicit

Those pupils who arrive at school with little in the way of literacy are unlikely to pick enough up unless we acknowledge that things we (and some of our pupils) just 'get' need to be explicitly taught. Some of these things are easy to miss because they seem so unutterably obvious. Every time you require pupils to read, write or speak, remember you are modelling literacy. If you're doing it consciously, you're much more likely to be doing it well. Take every opportunity to remind pupils how to do the things which are otherwise implicit.

Focus on high impact, low effort strategies

If it's easy, you're much more likely to try something. And if it works, you'll do it again. Avoid bolt-on literacy activities that have nothing to do with the subject you're teaching. Take every opportunity to teach the subject-specific language needed to read the texts you plan to study and the structure and form of the text types they need to write. Remember that there's absolutely no reason to get pupils to write letters pretending to be Marie Curie, newspaper reports on the Battle of Hastings or information leaflets explaining the properties of triangles to an alien. These activities are not literacy; they're a waste of valuable time and should be avoided.

Appendix 1
Slow Writing prompts

Your sentence will start with the word 'When'	Your sentence must be 23 words long
Your sentence will start with an adverb (usually ends in 'ly')	Your sentence must be a (rhetorical) question
Your sentence will address the second person, 'you'	Your sentence will include a quote
Your sentence will have 17 words in it	Your sentence will include an 'expert' opinion
Your sentence will have three words in it	Your sentence will contain alliteration
Your sentence will start with a word ending in 'ed'	Your sentence will contain brackets
Your sentence will include a simile	Your sentence will start with the word 'And'
Your sentence will have nine words in it	Your sentence will include a metaphor
Your sentence must contain a semicolon	Your sentence will have at least two commas in it
Your sentence must contain a colon	Your sentence will include a colour
Your sentence will have seven words in it	Your sentence will start with a word beginning with 'E'
Your sentence will start with the word 'Because'	Your sentence will be only one word!
Your sentence will start with the word 'Despite'	Your sentence will start with a word beginning with 'L'

Your sentence will include speech	Your sentence will end in an exclamation mark!
Your sentence will start with the word 'Below'	Your sentence will contain a rule of three
Your sentence will include a clause that starts with the word 'although'	Your sentence will start with a word beginning with 'R'
Your sentence will be 20 words exactly	Your sentence must start with a present participle (that's a verb ending in 'ing')

Appendix 2
Functional grammar

One way to successfully teach the academic literacy of our subjects is to use functional grammar. It's worth noting that functional grammar is something quite distinct from plain old vanilla grammar, which is more concerned with teaching word classes and sentence structure. Functional grammar is more about the 'actual meaning' of texts and sees language as systems rather than rules. It can be hugely useful in teaching academic language in a way that parallels the ways in which we naturally learn to speak in 'everyday' language.

The word-rich may arrive at secondary school with a good implicit understanding of traditional grammar and may well know many of the meta-linguistic terms we use to discuss language (noun, conjunction, clause) but not so the word-poor. For these pupils there is a disconnect between the way they use language and how they need to use it to succeed in school.

Functional grammar, or the systemic functional linguistics (SFL) theory of language and meaning, is the brainchild of professor of linguistics, Michael Halliday. SFL theory links language forms directly with the meanings they present, and offers ways of talking about language that can help learners to directly relate to language and content.

Michael Halliday proposed two levels of context: the context of culture, which he called 'genre', and the context of situation, or 'register'.[1]

Genres are about how we get things done. The genre of a text or communication is determined by its purpose and there are as many different genres as there are social purposes. Genres are predictable, patterned ways of using language and can, in the context of academic disciplines, be taught explicitly to pupils.

....

1   Michael Halliday and Jim Martin, *Continuum Companion to Systemic Functional Linguistics* (London: Continuum, 1993), p. 160.

The register of a text is broken down into three main areas: the *field* (*what* the communication is about), the *tenor* (*who* is taking part in the communication) and the *mode* (*how* things are being communicated).

John Polias calls this 'the register continuum'.[2] He argues that language is divided into three categories of register: everyday (informal), neutral (specialised) and academic (formal).

Informal register

- Field: stuff everyone knows.

- Tenor: the way that people who know each other really well talk.

- Mode: chatting.

Neutral register

- Field: stuff shared by distinct interest groups (e.g. gardening, mountain biking, computer games).

- Tenor: the way you might communicate with someone you've never met before.

- Mode: explaining experiences that are not shared.

2   John Polias, *Language and Learning in the KLAs and the Implications for Curriculum Writers* (Wayville, SA: Lexis Education, 2004), p. 3.

Academic register

- Field: stuff that's specific to particular subjects or disciplines.

- Tenor: institutional, impersonal communication.

- Mode: hypothetical, theoretical or encyclopaedic.

What we should be trying to do is move pupils' use of language from the informal and everyday, where they will feel comfortable, to the formal and academic, where they won't.

Of course, that doesn't mean the right-hand side of the continuum represents 'better' use of language. It merely represents how language is used in academic disciplines. Using language from the left-hand side at home, in the community and in other informal situations is perfectly acceptable. But many pupils don't have the ability to use language like this. And if we don't teach them to do this, no one will.

Appendix 3
Genre pedagogy

Communication is dependent on context. Within a particular context the language we use will usually follow predictable rules or conventions. These contextual uses of language are also referred to as genres. The idea is that if you're part of a group, you'll have no trouble recognising the conventions of the texts that other members of the group use routinely. Successful communication is about anticipating your reader or listener, and using genres helps to make what we're trying to communicate more predictable. For example, we're able to use contextual clues to work out very quickly whether a text is a joke, an advert or tax demand and respond appropriately. Genres are ways of getting things done or achieving social purposes.

Briefly, the idea is that learning to write involves learning how to use language. Genre pedagogy is an attempt to teach the written genres that occur in school subjects; it is teachers explaining the purpose, structure and grammar of a text, deconstructing models and then scaffolding their attempts to write their own texts. There are lots of different 'genre pedagogies' out there, but the one I've used is known as the Sydney School, or systemic functional linguistics, and is based on Michael Halliday's theories of functional grammar (see Appendix 2). Its chief architect, Professor Jim Martin of the University of Sydney, summarises his ideas about a language-based approach to teaching in *Learning to Write, Reading to Learn*.[1]

Martin and his colleagues identified the most common written genres of each school subject or discipline at each stage of schooling. From this they were able to map out a taxonomy of school genres which identified the main forms of writing that pupils most need to be able to use.

---

1   Jim R. Martin and David Rose, *Learning to Write, Reading to Learn: Genre, Knowledge and Pedagogy in the Sydney School* (London: Equinox Publishing, 2012).

These are:

1. Procedure: how something is done.

2. Description: what some particular thing is like.

3. Report: what an entire class of things is like.

4. Explanation: reasons why a judgement has been made.

5. Exposition: arguments why a thesis has been proposed.

Here are some examples of how purpose, structure and grammar fit into different genres:

A procedure

- Purpose – Tells us how to do something.

- Structure – Starts with the goal and then describes the materials needed and steps required.

- Grammar – Uses imperatives, action verbs, adjectives and adverbials to express details of time, place and manner, connectives and sequencers.

A report

- Purpose – Provides information on a subject.

- Structure – Starts with an identifying statement and then describes the subject.

- Grammar – Contains general nouns, relating verbs, action verbs, timeless present tense, topic sentences to organise bundles of information.[2]

This will look familiar to English teachers and, indeed, genre pedagogy is the root of what became debased as Writing Triplets and Genre, Audience and Purpose (GAP). The main difference is the focus on the grammar needed to write in particular genres.

Genres and language development are absolutely integral to pupils learning the knowledge of any discipline. Working with a focus on genre enables teachers to plan how to systematically teach the necessary language features of a text whilst explicitly pushing pupils away from using everyday language and enabling them to control academic language.

For examples of how these genres break down in geography, history and science, see: <http://www.slideshare.net/didau/genres-in-geography-history-and-science>.

---

2   Adapted from Ken Hyland, Genre Pedagogy: Language, Literacy and L2 Writing Instruction, *Journal of Second Language Writing* 6 (2007): 148–164, at p. 153.

References

All websites last accessed 22 October 2013.

Alexander, Robin (2012) *Improving Oracy and Classroom Talk in English Schools: Achievements and Challenges* (Cambridge: Cambridge University Press).

Banyai, Istvan (2012) Why Writers Should Learn Math, *The New Yorker* (2 November). Available at: <http://www.newyorker.com/online/blogs/books/2012/11/writers-should-learn-math.html>.

Barbash, Shepard (2011) *Clear Teaching: With Direct Instruction, Siegfried Engelmann Discovered a Better Way of Teaching* [ebook] (Arlington, VA: Education Consumers Foundation).

Barton, Geoff (2010) Whatever Your Subject, You Are a Teacher of English, *Times Educational Supplement* (5 March). Available at: <http://www.tes.co.uk/article.aspx?storycode=6038152>.

Barton, Geoff (2013) *Don't Call It Literacy! What Every Teacher Needs to Know about Speaking, Listening, Reading and Writing* (London: Routledge/David Fulton).

Beadle, Phil (2010) *How to Teach* (Carmarthen: Crown House Publishing).

Beck, Isabel, Margaret McKeown and **Linda Kucan** (2013) *Bringing Words to Life: Robust Vocabulary Instruction*, 2nd edn (New York: Guilford Press).

Beere, Jackie (2010) *The Perfect Ofsted Lesson* (Carmarthen: Crown House Publishing).

Berger, Ron (2003) *An Ethic of Excellence: Building a Culture of Craftsmanship with Students* (Portsmouth, NH: Heinemann Educational Books).

Berger, Ron (2012) Ron Berger on Critique, Part 2 [video] (1 December). Available at: <http://howtovideos.hightechhigh.org/video/275/Ron+Berger+on+Critique+part+2+of+2>.

Biemiller, Andrew (2003) Vocabulary: Needed If More Children Are To Read Well, *Reading Psychology* 24(3–4): 323–335.

Bjork, Robert A. (n.d.) Long-Term Memory [video]. Available at: <http://gocognitive.net/interviews/retrieval-induced-forgetting>.

Bjork, Robert A. (2013) Desirable Difficulties Perspective on Learning. In H. Pashler (ed.), *Encyclopedia of the Mind* (Thousand Oaks, CA: Sage Reference). Available at: <http://bjorklab.psych.ucla.edu/pubs/RBjork_inpress.pdf>.

Bourdieu, Pierre (1986) The Forms of Capital. In John G. Richardson (ed.), *Handbook of Theory and Research for the Sociology of Education* (New York: Greenwood), pp. 241–258.

Britton, James (1970) *Language and Learning* (Harmondsworth: Penguin).

Christodoulou, Daisy (2013) *Seven Myths about Education* [ebook] (London: The Curriculum Centre).

Coffin, Caroline (2006) Learning the Language of School History: The Role of Linguistics in Mapping the Writing Demands of the Secondary School Curriculum, *Journal of Curriculum Studies* 38(4): 413–429.

Corbett, Pie and **Julia Strong** (2011) *Talk for Writing across the Curriculum* (Milton Keynes: Open University Press).

Csikszentmihalyi, Mihaly (1990) *Flow: The Psychology of Optimal Experience* (New York: Harper and Row).

De La Paz, Susan and **Mark Felton** (2010) Reading and Writing from Multiple Source Documents in History: Effects of Strategy Instruction With Low to Average High School Writers, *Contemporary Educational Psychology* 35(3): 313–300.

Department for Education (2012) Encouraging Reading for Pleasure (25 June). Available at: <http://www.education.gov.uk/schools/teachingandlearning/pedagogy/b00192950/encouraging-reading-for-pleasure>.

Department for Children, Schools and Families (2008) *The National Strategies – Primary. Talk for Writing in Practice: The Teaching Sequence for Writing.* Ref: 00467-2008PDF-EN-21. Available at: <http://www.teachfind.com/national-strategies/teaching-sequence-writing-0>.

Department for Education (2012) *Teachers' Standards.* Ref: DFE-00066-2011. Available at: <https://www.education.gov.uk/publications/eOrderingDownload/teachers%20standards.pdf>.

Didau, David (2012) *The Perfect (Ofsted) English Lesson* (Carmarthen: Independent Thinking Press).

Dweck, Carol (2006) *Mindset: The New Psychology of Success* (New York: Random House).

References

Engelmann, Siegfried (1982) *Theory of Instruction: Principles and Applications* (Eugene, OR: ADI Press).

Ericsson, K. Anders, Michael J. Prietula and **Edward T. Cokely** (2007) The Making of an Expert, *Harvard Business Review* (July–August). Available at: <http://www.uvm.edu/~pdodds/files/papers/others/2007/ericsson2007a.pdf>.

European Commission (2012) *EU High Level Group of Experts on Literacy: Final Report* (September). Available at: <http://ec.europa.eu/education/literacy/resources/final-report/index_en.htm>.

Fearn, Leif and **Nancy Farnan** (1997) *Writing Effectively: Helping Children Master the Conventions of Writing* (Boston, MA: Allyn and Bacon).

Feez, Susan (1998) *Text-Based Syllabus Design* (Sydney: McQuarie University/AMES).

Flint, David, Lindsay Frost, Simon Oakes, et al. (2009) *Edexcel GCSE Geography B: Evolving Planet Student Book* (Harlow: Pearson Education).

Ramsay Fowler, H., Jane E. Aaron and **Kay Limburg** (1995) *The Little, Brown Handbook*, 6th edn (New York: HarperCollins).

Gibbons, Pauline (2002) *Scaffolding Language, Scaffolding Learning: Teaching Second Language Learners in the Mainstream Classroom* (Portsmouth, NH: Heinemann Educational Books).

Gladwell, Malcolm (2008) *Outliers: The Story of Success* (London: Penguin).

Gove, Michael (2011) We Must Teach Our Children to Love Books Again, *The Telegraph* (31 March). Available at: <http://www.telegraph.co.uk/education/8419855/We-must-teach-our-children-to-love-books-again.html>.

Guardian, The (2012) Literary Non-Fiction: The Facts (21 September). Available at: <http://www.theguardian.com/books/2012/sep/21/literary-nonfiction-the-facts>.

Gwynne, N. M. (2013) *Gwynne's Grammar: The Ultimate Introduction to Grammar and the Writing of Good English* (London: Ebury Press).

Halliday, Michael and **Jim Martin** (1993) *Continuum Companion to Systemic Functional Linguistics* (London: Continuum).

Halliday, Michael and **Christian Matthiessan** (2004) *An Introduction to Functional Grammar* (London: Hodder Education).

Hardy, Godfrey H. (1941) *A Mathematician's Apology* (Cambridge: Cambridge University Press).

Hattie, John (2009) *Visible Learning: A Synthesis of Over 800 Meta-Analyses Relating to Achievement* (London: Routledge).

Hattie, John (2012) *Visible Learning for Teachers: Maximizing Impact on Learning* (London: Routledge).

Hattie, John and **Gregory Yates** (2013) *Visible Learning and the Science of How We Learn* (London: Routledge).

Hirsch, Eric Donald, Jr (1999) *The Schools We Need: And Why We Don't Have Them* (New York: Anchor Books).

Hirsch, Eric Donald, Jr (2007) *The Knowledge Deficit: Closing the Shocking Education Gap for American Children* (Boston, MA: Houghton Mifflin).

Hyland, Ken (2004) *Genre and Second Language Writing* (Ann Arbor, MI: University of Michigan Press).

Hyland, Ken (2007) Genre Pedagogy: Language, Literacy and L2 Writing Instruction, *Journal of Second Language Writing* 6: 148–164.

Jama, Deeqa and **George Dugdale** (2010) *Literacy: State of the Nation: A Picture of Literacy in the UK Today* (London: National Literacy Trust).

Kerr, Hugo (2008) *The Cognitive Psychology of Literacy Teaching: Reading, Writing, Spelling, Dyslexia (and a Bit Besides)* [ebook]. Available at: <http://www.hugokerr.info/book.pdf>.

King, Stephen (2000) *On Writing: A Memoir* (London: Hodder and Stoughton).

Kirby, Joe (2013) *How to Start on Teach First* [Kindle edn] (London: Teach First).

Kirby, Joe (2013) *How to Start on Teach First: English* [Kindle edn] (London: Teach First).

Kolata, Gina (2012) Genes Now Tell Doctors Secrets They Can't Utter, *New York Times* (25 August). Available at: <http://www.nytimes.com/2012/08/26/health/research/with-rise-of-gene-sequencing-ethical-puzzles.html?pagewanted=all&_r=0>.

Kornell, Nate and **Robert A. Bjork** (2007) Learning Concepts and Categories: Is Spacing the 'Enemy of Induction'? *Psychological Science* 19(6): 585–592.

Laing, Aislinn (2010) Teenagers 'Only Use 800 Different Words A Day', *The Telegraph* (11 January). Available at: <http://www.telegraph.co.uk/education/educationnews/6960745/Teenagers-only-use-800-different-words-a-day.html>.

Lane, Peter and **Christopher Lane** (1992) *History: Key Stage 3 Study Guides* (London: Letts Educational).

Lemov, Doug (2010) *Teach Like A Champion: 49 Techniques that Put Students on the Path to College* (San Francisco, CA: Jossey-Bass).

Lemov, Doug, Erica Woolway and **Katie Yezzi** (2012) *Practice Perfect: 42 Rules for Getting Better at Getting Better* (San Francisco, CA: Jossey-Bass).

Mansell, Warwick (2008) Pupil–Teacher Interaction, *TES* (21 November). Available at: <http://www.tes.co.uk/article.aspx?storycode=6005411>.

Martin, Jim R. and **David Rose** (2012) *Learning to Write, Reading to Learn: Genre, Knowledge and Pedagogy in the Sydney School* (London: Equinox Publishing).

McCardle, Peggy, Hollis Scarborough and **Hugh Catts** (2001) Predicting, Explaining, and Preventing Children's Reading Difficulties, *Learning Disabilities Research and Practice* 16(4): 230–239.

Myhill, Debra and **Ros Fisher** (2005) *Informing Practice in English: A Review of Recent Research in Literacy and the Teaching of English* (London: Ofsted).

Nater, Swen and **Ronald Gallimore** (2005) *You Haven't Taught Until They Have Learned: John Wooden's Teaching Principles and Practices* (Morgantown, WV: Fitness Information Technology).

Norton, Elizabeth and **Maryanne Wolf** (2012) Rapid Automatized Naming (RAN) and Reading Fluency: Implications for Understanding and Treatment of Reading Disabilities. *Annual Review of Psychology* 63: 427–452.

Nuthall, Graham (2005) The Cultural Myths and Realities of Classroom Teaching and Learning: A Personal Journey, *Teachers College Record* 107: 895–934.

Nuthall, Graham (2007) *The Hidden Lives of Learners* (Wellington: New Zealand Council of Educational Research).

Nystrand, Martin (1997) *Opening Dialogue: Understanding the Dynamics of Language and Learning in the English Classroom* (New York: Teachers College Press).

Ofsted (2011) *Reading, Writing and Communication (Literacy): Distance Learning Materials for Inspection within the New Framework*. Ref: 110125. Available at: <http://www.ofsted.gov.uk/resources/reading-writing-and-communication-literacy>.

Ofsted (2011) *Removing Barriers to Literacy*. Ref: 090237. Available at: <http://www.ofsted.gov.uk/resources/removing-barriers-literacy>.

Ofsted (2012) *Moving English Forward*. Ref: 110118. Available at: <http://www.ofsted.gov.uk/resources/moving-english-forward>.

Ofsted (2013) *The Framework for School Inspection*. Ref: 120100. Available at: <http://www.ofsted.gov.uk/resources/framework-for-school-inspection>.

Ofsted (2013) *Improving Literacy in Secondary Schools: A Shared Responsibility*. Ref: 120363. Available at: <http://www.ofsted.gov.uk/resources/improving-literacy-secondary-schools-shared-responsibility>.

Polias, John (2004) *Language and Learning in the KLAs and the Implications for Curriculum Writers* (Wayville, SA: Lexis Education).

Polias, John (2006) Assessing Learning: A Language-Based Approach. I Symposium. Available at: <http://www.su.se/polopoly_fs/1.84020.1333710072!/menu/standard/file/2006_3_Polias.pdf>.

Richland, Lindsey E., Robert A. Bjork, Jason R. Finley and **Marcia C. Linn** (2005) Linking Cognitive Science to Education: Generation and Interleaving Effects. In B. G. Bara, L. Barsalou and M. Bucciarelli (eds), *Proceedings of the Twenty-Seventh Annual Conference of the Cognitive Science Society* (Mahwah, NJ: Lawrence Erlbaum), pp. 1850–1855.

Rigney, Daniel (2010) *The Matthew Effect: How Advantage Begets Further Advantage* (New York: Columbia University Press).

Robinson, Ken (2006) How Schools Kill Creativity [video]. Available at: <http://www.ted.com/talks/ken_robinson_says_schools_kill_creativity.html>.

Robinson, Ken (2010) Changing Education Paradigms [video]. Available at: <http://www.ted.com/talks/ken_robinson_changing_education_paradigms.html>.

Robinson, Martin (2013) *Trivium 21c: Preparing Young People for the Future with Lessons from the Past* (Carmarthen: Crown House Publishing).

Rose, David and **Jim Martin** (2012) *Learning to Write/Reading to Learn: Genre, Knowledge and Pedagogy in the Sydney School: Scaffolding Democracy in Literacy Classrooms* (Sheffield: Equinox Publishing).

Sampson, George (1921) *English for the English: A Chapter on National Education* (Cambridge: Cambridge University Press).

Scarborough, Hollis S. (2001) Connecting Early Language and Literacy to Later Reading (Dis)Abilities: Evidence, Theory, and Practice. In Susan B. Neuman and David K. Dickinson (eds), *Handbook of Early Literacy Research, Volume 1* (New York: Guilford Press, 2001).

Sedgwick, Marcus (2007) *My Swordhand is Singing* (London: Orion Children's Books).

Smith, Jim (2009) *The Lazy Teacher's Handbook* (Carmarthen: Crown House Publishing).

Strunk, William, Jr (2011 [1918]) *The Elements of Style* [ebook] (n.p.: Tribeca Books).

Swan, Michael (2005) *Practical English Usage*, 3rd rev. edn (Oxford: Oxford University Press).

Vygotsky, Lev (1978) *Mind in Society: The Development of Higher Psychological Processes*, new edn (Cambridge, MA: Harvard University Press).

Vygotsky, Lev (2012 [1962]) *Thought and Language* (Cambridge, MA: MIT Press).

Wiliam, Dylan (2007) Assessment, Learning and Technology: Prospects at the Periphery of Control. Keynote address at ALT-C, the 14th International Conference of the Association for Learning Technology, Nottingham, 4–6 September. Available at: <www.alt.ac.uk/docs/altc2007_dylan_wiliam_keynote_transcript.pdf>.

Wiliam, Dylan (2007) Keeping Learning on Track: Formative Assessment and the Regulation of Learning. In M. Coupland, J. Anderson and T. Spencer (eds), *Making Mathematics Vital: Proceedings of the Twentieth Biennial Conference of the Australian Association of Mathematics Teachers* (Adelaide: Australian Association of Mathematics Teachers Inc.), pp. 20–34.

Wiliam, Dylan (2011) *Embedded Formative Assessment* (Bloomington, IN: Solution Tree Press).

Wiliam, Dylan (2013) Principles of Curriculum Design. Presentation delivered at the SSAT Conference on Principled Curriculum Design: Tools for Schools, Manchester, 8 March. Available at: <http://www.redesigningschooling.org.uk/wp-content/uploads/2012/11/Dylan-Curriculum-Presentation.pdf>.

Wilkinson, Andrew (1965) The Concept of Oracy, *English in Education* 2(A2) (June): 3–5.

Willingham, Daniel (2009) *Why Don't Students Like School? A Cognitive Scientist Answers Questions About How the Mind Works and What It Means for the Classroom* (San Francisco, CA: Wiley).

Wood, David, Jerome Bruner and **Gail Ross** (1970) *The Role of Tutoring in Problem Solving* (Oxford: Pergamon Press).

Blogs

Lisa Ashes, *The Learning Geek* – thelearninggeek.com

Daisy Christodoulou, *The Curriculum Centre* – www.thecurriculumcentre.org/blog

Chris Curtis, *Learning from My Mistakes: An English Teacher's Blog* –learningfrom-mymistakesenglish.blogspot.co.uk

Lee Donaghy, *What's Language Doing Here?* – whatslanguagedoinghere.wordpress.com

Zoë Elder, *Full On Learning* – fullonlearning.com

Harry Fletcher-Wood, *Improving Teaching* – improvingteaching.co.uk

Joe Kirby, *Back to the Whiteboard* – back2thewhiteboard.wordpress.com

Darren Mead, *Sharing Pedagogical Purposes* – pedagogicalpurposes.blogspot.co.uk

Kenny Pieper, *Just Trying To Be Better Than Yesterday* – justtryingtobebetter.net

Kerry Pulleyn, *The Plenary* – theplenary.wordpress.com

Alex Quigley, *Hunting English* – www.huntingenglish.com

Martin Robinson, *Surreal Anarchy* – martinrobborobinson.wordpress.com

John Sayers, *John Sayers Geography Blog* – sayersjohn.blogspot.co.uk

Tom Sherrington, *Headguruteacher* – headguruteacher.com

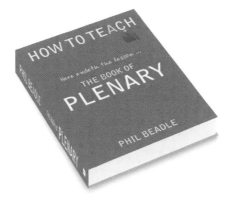

978-1-78135-053-9

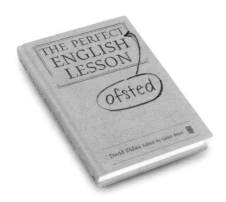

978-1-78135-052-2

www.independentthinkingpress.com

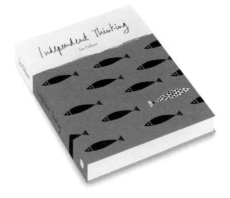

978-1-78135-055-3

978-1-78135-108-6

 www.independentthinkingpress.com